## Praise for *The Six* ............ .... .. ...
## the Resources Your School Community Needs

Luis Torres has a passion for fairness, equity, students, and their families that is evident throughout his new book, *The Six Priorities.* As an early proponent of the community school model, I have long believed that we must foster strong collaborations between schools, social service agencies, and health professionals in communities that are plagued by poverty. *The Six Priorities* provides practical, proven strategies to build community partnerships that have been shown to improve student outcomes. It is a must-read for any education professional who seeks to build a more just and equitable world for our children.

—Dr. Betty A. Rosa
*Commissioner of Education and President*
*of the University of the State of New York*

Today's school leaders are charged with doing more with less. Throughout his career, Luis Torres has been relentless in accessing "village" resources to ensure that students reach their preferred futures. *The Six Priorities* serves as a blueprint for other school leaders striving to secure strategic partnerships to close the gaps and remove barriers that threaten student success. Torres moves beyond the *why* and *what* of community schools to the *how* with purpose and urgency.

—Cheryl Watson-Harris
*Co-Founder, Urban School Specialists, LLC*

Never was the need for an "edulution" more important than now. Mr. Torres brilliantly gives us not only the "why" but also the "how" to ensure that education is priority number 1 for everyone. In *The Six Priorities*, Mr. Torres writes from a place of hope, passion, and commitment to making education an equitable enterprise. He lays out a structure with very clear steps for following and developing a community school model. He is a brilliant storyteller, a transformational leader, and an advocate for changing the way we think about our schools in our communities. He has given us a playbook, and we should all take up his charge and become "equity warriors"!

—Dr. Barbara McKeon
*Senior Program Director, Cahn Fellows Program,*
*and 2015 Cahn Fellow for Distinguished Principals*

# THE SIX PRIORITIES

# THE SIX PRIORITIES

## How to Find the Resources Your School Community Needs

**Luis Eladio Torres**

Arlington, Virginia USA

2800 Shirlington Road, Suite 1001 • Arlington, VA 22206 USA
Phone: 800-933-2723 or 703-578-9600 • Fax: 703-575-5400
Website: www.ascd.org • Email: member@ascd.org
Author guidelines: www.ascd.org/write

Penny Reinart, *Deputy Executive Director*; Genny Ostertag, *Managing Director, Book Acquisitions & Editing*; Allison Scott, *Senior Acquisitions Editor*; Mary Beth Nielsen, *Director, Book Editing*; Miriam Calderone, *Editor*; Thomas Lytle, *Creative Director*; Donald Ely, *Art Director*; Lindsey Smith/The Hatcher Group, *Graphic Designer*; Keith Demmons, *Senior Production Designer*; Circle Graphics, *Typesetter*; Kelly Marshall, *Production Manager*; Shajuan Martin, *E-Publishing Specialist*

PAPERBACK ISBN: 978-1-4166-3155-2    ASCD product #122022                      n1/23
PDF E-BOOK ISBN: 978-1-4166-3156-9; see Books in Print for other formats.
Quantity discounts are available: email programteam@ascd.org or call 800-933-2723, ext. 5773, or 703-575-5773. For desk copies, go to www.ascd.org/deskcopy.

**Library of Congress Cataloging-in-Publication Data**

Names: Torres, Luis Eladio, author.
Title: The six priorities : how to find the resources your school community
   needs / Luis Eladio Torres.
Other titles: 6 priorities
Description: Arlington, VA : ASCD, [2023] | Includes bibliographical
   references and index.
Identifiers: LCCN 2022034213 (print) | LCCN 2022034214 (ebook) |
   ISBN 9781416631552 (Paperback) | ISBN 9781416631569 (pdf)
Subjects: LCSH: Community schools–United States. | Community and
   school–United States. | Food security–United States. |
   Dwellings–Social aspects–United States. | Community-based child
   welfare–United States. | Quality of life–Health aspects. | Educational
   technology–United States. | Students with social
   disabilities–Education–United States.
Classification: LCC LB2820 .T67 2023  (print) | LCC LB2820  (ebook) |
   DDC 371.03–dc23/eng/20220831
LC record available at https://lccn.loc.gov/2022034213
LC ebook record available at https://lccn.loc.gov/2022034214

31 30 29 28 27 26 25 24 23      1 2 3 4 5 6 7 8 9 10 11 12

*I dedicate this book to my father, Luis Angel Torres, for making me the man I am today and for his 45 years of service to the Bronx.*

*Also to my mother, Elizabeth Torres, for bringing me into this world and providing me with a great childhood.*

*Finally, to my wife, Joan; my three children, Autumn, Isiah, and Sienna; and the rest of my family, for supporting me in doing the work necessary to end the inequities of the world.*

## How to Find the Resources
## Your School Community Needs

# Acknowledgments

I would like to thank Allison Scott and Miriam Calderone from ASCD for helping me to write my first book.

I would like to express my deepest appreciation to Stephen Rappaport for believing in me and nominating me to the NYC Leadership Academy. You will always be family to me. I would also like to thank the Watson family for helping to mold me and supporting my efforts.

I am grateful to Amy Andino, David Banks, Abe Barretto, Artie Cahn, Mark Cannizzaro, Elizabeth Cedeno, Michelle Centeno, Jo Champa, Venanzio Ciampa, Dolores Esposito, Juanita Feliciano, Abe Fernandez, Commissioner Ramon Garcia, Ramon Gonzalez, Sandra Gonzalez, Cheryl Watson Harris, Amee Hernandez, Cynthia Jones, A. Carole Joseph, Michael Kohlhagen, Mac McDonald, Barbara McKeon, Ray Negron, Kaisa Newhams (Project Santa), Anthony Orzo, Arelis Parachi, Janet Patti, Jeff Piontek, Cynthia Pond, Meisha Porter, Dr. Betty A. Rosa, Denise Schira, Harry Sherman, Bob Spata, Sandra Stein, Brandon Steiner, Ron Sussman, Steve Sussman, Ken Thompson, Ed Tom, Rose Trentman, Ben Waxman, Cheryl Wills, Lew Zuchman, and my NYCESPA family for being mentors to me.

I am also grateful to Karim Abouelnaga, Jason Acosta, David Aviles, Mario Benabe, Christina DeJesus, Gabriel DeJesus, Musu Drammeh, Miguel Flores, Leroy Freeman, Jay Pierre Ithier, and Community School 55 staff for always supporting the work and being family to me.

Special thanks to the elected officials of the Bronx, especially Jaamal Bailey, Michael Blake, Jaamal Bowman, Marcos Crespo, Rubén Díaz Jr., Vanessa L. Gibson, Chantel Jackson, Latoya Joyner, Gustavo Rivera, Rafael Salamanca, and Althea Stevens.

I would like to extend my sincere thanks to all my partners in this work, including Arc of Justice (Kirsten Foy, Phil Gates, CB Gray, and Fritz Penn), ASCD, the Bronx Children's Museum, Bronx Crypto, the Bronx Zoo, BronxNet (Michael Max Knobbe), Bulova, Cahn Fellows, the Center for Educational Innovation, the City College of New York, CSA, Cultural African Preservation, Early Reading Matters, Education Through Music, Educators for Student Success Association, Fordham University, Furacao Capoeira, Graham Windham, Green Bronx Machine (Stephen and Lizette Ritz), Healthfirst, Hostos Community College, Hunter College, Josh Johnson, Learning Ally, Lehman College, Mercy College, Montefiore Hospital, New York Cares, the New York City Elementary School Principals Association, the New York City Fire Department, the New York City Police Department (Lt. Perez and Det. Washington), the New York Junior Tennis League, the New York Yankees, Practice Makes Perfect, Puerto Rican Flags Up, Scan_Harbor, Soles4Souls (Tiffany Turner), Street Soccer USA, TEQ, Wellness in the Schools, and Windows of Hip Hop (Melissa Libran, Paul La Salle, Bronx Mama, Grandmaster CAZ, and Grandmaster Melle Mel).

# Introduction

Here is a harsh truth that many educators need to recognize: for many families with children, education is not their first priority; it is the *sixth* priority, after food, shelter, safety, health, and access to technology. It's not that families do not value education. Rather, life's challenges and people's basic needs overshadow school as a priority. Families must make hard decisions on whether to feed their children, pay the rent, fill a prescription, or purchase school materials. In the end, life's necessities will win. And from the school's perspective, before thinking about instruction, assessment, classroom manage-ment, and other aspects of education, educators must find resources to support families in addressing the priorities that are fundamental to their well-being.

As an educator, you see how these priorities affect your students. Access to food—especially healthy food—is often limited, and many children don't eat three meals a day. Many families suffer from problems with housing, whether it is homelessness or generally poor living conditions. Children in many neighborhoods face constant trauma, as they are exposed to violence and other issues that threaten their safety. Illnesses and chronic diseases may be untreated if the community lacks hospitals, medical and dental clinics, and other health-care providers. Without access to technology such as laptops and affordable internet service, students may be unable to fully participate in school assignments, and their families may be left without easy access to helpful community resources. Children who are hungry, homeless or poorly housed, scared, unhealthy, and lacking easy access to technology may find it difficult to focus on school. Poverty is not an excuse. It is something that we must acknowledge and work on by seeking real solutions to fill the gaps that it creates.

In this book, I will identify many of the challenges our families face and provide proven ways to address them through the development of community schools. I will help you to make education the *first* priority by addressing the other five basic needs and providing you with a process that will help you to secure the resources you need to better serve your community and to reduce the inequities that exist throughout our society.

## Inequities

Poverty is not an incurable disease but a failure of society to provide an equitable living situation for all. We must fight the inequities of the world, stamp out poverty through education, and provide our communities with the resources they need.

Inequities do not exist because of broken systems. The systems were created for a purpose, and I believe they are doing exactly what they were created to do—to get different outcomes for different people. For example, have you ever noticed that when a school that is labeled as "failing" begins to improve, funds that helped them to improve are cut? I view this as a systemic way to keep schools and organizations in a state of failure. Similarly, the characterization of many schools as "pipelines to prison" because of discriminatory discipline practices reflects the fact that for many students—especially Black and Brown students—their school experience is more likely to lead to imprisonment than to college, a situation that is unacceptable. We need to become "plumbers" and dismantle that pipeline.

For many years, I have been calling on people to rise up and begin an "edulution." You could define "edulution" as an education *revolution,* or as an *evolution* of education. The world needs to evolve, and education needs a great deal of development and innovation if we are to change the negative outcomes affecting many of our organizations and communities. It is important that we fight for equity for all, and I believe college should be free for everyone.

To change the world in a broader sense, we must change mindsets. It is easier to educate and help people when they know that they have a chance at a better life, when they believe they can be successful and attain equal access to life's necessities. Family income or zip code should not determine quality of life. When people believe they can win in life, they work harder. The more we develop positive mindsets, the better communities will become. We need to raise the standards for our children and communities so that people feel a sense of pride and are willing to work to sustain and improve their environments.

## Where I'm Coming From

Growing up, I did not know about the inequities of the world. I thought that I had the ability to be as successful as anyone else. It was not until high school that I realized how unfair this world is. In high school, my guidance counselor told me to join the military because she did not believe that I would be successful in college. She never took the time to get acquainted with me as an individual or to learn about my creative abilities. I was a talented artist, and my grades were not so bad. If she had recommended that I apply to a college with a focus on the arts, I believe I would have been successful. Sadly, that was not the case, and I enlisted in the Navy at age 18. It was then that I made a commitment to myself that I would never allow anyone else to tell me what I could or could not do in life.

After completing Naval boot camp in 1990, I came back to New York to attend college. I earned an associate's degree in science from Hostos Community College, a bachelor's degree in child psychology from the City College of New York, and a master's degree in education from Mercy College—proving that guidance counselor wrong. I became a successful teacher, but I soon realized that the position gave me only limited ability to have an impact on the greater community. I decided to attend Hunter College, where I earned an advanced degree in school administration. I thought this degree would lead automatically to selection as a school administrator, but again I had to work twice as hard to get to where I needed to go. So I enlisted in the New York City Leadership Academy, which led directly to my appointment in 2004 as principal of C.S. 55 Benjamin Franklin, one of the most challenging schools in the city. I am happy to say that many positive changes have occurred at the school during my tenure.

Unfortunately, more than 30 years after my guidance counselor told me I would not be successful in college, I witnessed history repeating itself. My daughter, who is an excellent student, recently applied for admission to a state university that specializes in the arts. I thought that her admission would be a sure thing, but she was not accepted. Doing some follow-up research on admission statistics, I found that foreign students are more likely to be admitted than Black or Brown American students. As a taxpaying resident of the state and a military veteran, I was upset that my daughter was denied access to the school. In my mind, the rejection of her application was an example of the many systemic inequities that continue to exist and that we must fight.

# Becoming an Equity Warrior

Your community and the children you serve need you now more than ever. It is important that you leverage your partners, friends, and family members to do this challenging work. As an educator, you must become an "equity warrior" who is willing to fight for your school community and help your families gain access to the resources they need. Using the community-matching process described in Chapter 1 and further elaborated on in Chapters 2 through 7, you can become a catalyst for change.

As you read this book and learn how to use the tools provided, you will have what you need to combat the inequities in your community. I have confidence that, together, we can make a difference. I will be your partner in this work.

## A Note on the Pandemic

The COVID-19 pandemic brought existing inequities into sharp relief and highlighted the need to strengthen resources for vulnerable communities. The need for community schools became even more evident. As schools across the United States closed, communities that were dependent on these schools for services beyond classroom instruction began to suffer disproportionately. Many people did not know how they could survive without the support the schools provided. The pandemic experience showed that many families rely on schools for food, shelter, safety, health, and access to technology.

In most chapters, you'll find a text box titled "What We Learned from the Pandemic." My hope is that the lessons learned during this crisis can help us be better prepared to deal with future crises.

# Community Schools and Community Matching

Community schools grew from a need for society to address the inequities that exist in many of our communities. Sadly, there are communities that do not have all the resources they need to be productive and safe living spaces. They do not have banks, hospitals, and stores that offer healthy foods. They have literally been abandoned by society. Community schools try to fill the gaps in this inequitable world. They aim to have an impact on the whole child and the whole community and are one of the major approaches to ensuring that all children have what they need to be successful in life. These schools seek solutions to societal needs so that our children can focus on education. My school, C.S. 55, is one of more than 300 community schools in New York City, all of which receive city, state, and federal funding.

A community school is a partnership between the school and various organizations to meet the needs of the community it serves. Its main purpose is to improve student academic performance by focusing on youth development, parent engagement, health and wellness, housing, mental health, culture, climate, attendance, and other areas of need. This model addresses the whole child by working with the whole community. A community school serves as the focal point for partners to provide services and opportunities for children and their families both during and after the school day.

Betty A. Rosa, the New York State commissioner of education, once said that the community school approach is crucial for boosting test scores at a school like C.S. 55. But she also said that test scores can't be the sole or even primary motivation for addressing students' mental, physical, and emotional needs. "The intent is not to push the needle on test scores," Dr. Rosa told me. "I think that when children are healthy, mentally ready, have had good entry points, have had a community that supports them—that prepares students to be ready."

When I started to develop my community school model at C.S. 55, the purpose was to address the needs of the whole child, with a focus on attendance. I quickly realized that I could not do this work without trying to address the inequities of the community, and so, over the years, my work has evolved in this direction. The school is now working with various partners, elected officials, and community members to address the needs of the surrounding community.

The community schools model reminds us that we must stop looking at school as an oasis. When we think of an oasis, most of us probably think of a patch of fertile land that is surrounded by areas with few, if any, signs of life. The oasis concept gives the impression that there are no resources for sustainability of life in the larger community. This is not an accurate depiction of what a community is, and it is unfair to the people who live there. A school and its surrounding community should be looked at as a rain forest—a place with vast resources inside and out. As community school leaders, we must look to our community for the resources our children need to be successful, and, if necessary, we should venture outside our community for additional supports.

By focusing on the five priorities of food, shelter, safety, health, and technology access, community schools are creating a support structure for addressing the sixth priority, education, and are helping to reduce the performance gap between students who live in wealthy communities and those who live in high-need areas. They have become a way to address the inequities of society. In the community school model at C.S. 55, addressing inequities involves a process I have developed called *community matching*.

## The Community-Matching Process

Community matching is a way to match the needs of the school community with the resources that are available within and beyond the school. Through this process, I have been able to secure more than $50 million in funds for C.S. 55, as well as for schools across the borough of the Bronx. Many schools have received funds for computer and science labs, schoolyard enhancements, technology upgrades, libraries, cafeterias, and auditoriums.

When implementing the community-matching process in your school, you need to work with people who know your community well, including parents and community leaders who can advise you on what resources the school truly needs in order to be successful. You want to make sure to provide things that match the needs of the community rather than things that might be nice to have but are unnecessary. Initiatives have failed because they do not have strong support from people in the community. These individuals will be crucial members of your leadership team and will help you gather information. Often, when I have to decide on a resource or program for C.S. 55, I count on parents, community leaders, and key people in the school to provide advice. Having the right people on your team makes it more likely that your effort will have a positive impact on the community.

The community-matching process involves four steps: (1) identifying the gaps, (2) specifying needs, (3) telling your story, and (4) establishing strategic partnerships. (In the following chapters, you will see how these steps also apply to the priorities of food, shelter, safety, health, access to technology, and education.) Figure 1.1 is a worksheet that incorporates these four steps. It will give you the structure you need to organize your thoughts and create your plan of action. It can be a framework or blueprint for requesting the funds you will need to support your organization (it is not intended to be a grant application). A blank downloadable PDF of the worksheet is available at www.ascd.org/torres-community-matching-worksheet.

**FIGURE 1.1**

---

## Community-Matching Worksheet

*Directions:* Use the questions in each section as prompts to help you complete the worksheet. (In the following chapters, you will find samples of completed worksheets for each of the priorities.)

### Identifying the Gaps

- What are the needs of your school community in this area?
- What are the resources your school offers to the community in this area?
- Where are the gaps?
- What resources does the surrounding community have to offer?

### Specifying Needs

- What does your school need to achieve its goals?
- What can you identify as being essential to your school's ability to function at a high level?

- What will make it much easier for you to do your job and improve your school and community?

<br><br><br><br><br><br>

## Telling Your Story

- What are your school's demographics?
- What are your school's needs in this area?
- What challenges does your school face in meeting those needs?
- What do you hope to accomplish through the proposed initiative/program?

<br><br><br><br><br><br>

## Establishing Strategic Partnerships

- Who are people you know who could help with this initiative/program?
- What organizations could help?

To complete the worksheet, you will need to answer a series of questions, which you can do with your team of staff and community members. The questions will require you to closely examine the needs of your community, families, and students, and to determine how you are going to address these needs. The starting point—identifying the gaps between needs and available resources—is critical. You cannot fix your problems without first identifying what the problems are. My hope is that when you have completed the process, you will not only have a plan of action to gain the resources you need but also better understand how to lead your organization.

## Identifying the Gaps

Identifying the gaps between what you need and the resources you have is the basis for developing your plan of action. In many places, schools have long failed to meet the needs of their communities. Systemic racism and inequities have contributed to this failure. Low-performing schools losing government funding when they reach a certain level of improvement is an example of how systems can work against success. This sad reality makes it important for us to find ways to get resources from various places so that we are no longer totally dependent on funds from the city, state, or federal government. Advocating for resources is not optional. It is an absolute necessity if we are to combat the inequities of the world.

## Specifying Needs

Once you have identified the gaps, you can focus on those things that your school community needs. If you do not know what you need, you cannot ask for it, and if you don't know what to ask for, people will not invest in your effort. You must identify and prioritize your needs before you can ask for resources or apply for grants. Every funder or possible partner will want to know what it is you actually need to address the deficiencies of your school and community. Does your organization need a technology upgrade? Do you need to install air conditioning in your auditorium? Do you need to relocate your cafeteria? Does your schoolyard need safety improvements? Do you need funding for a music program?

You can begin by creating a wish list, but then, as mentioned earlier, you must review it carefully to identify which items are things that you actually *need* and separate them from things you *want*. Just because you want something does not mean you need it. A want may be a cosmetic thing that will make something look better but is not strictly necessary. For example, you might want to beautify a public space, but is this something you need to help achieve the organization's goals? Needs are things you can identify as being essential to your school's ability to function at a high level. They should make it much easier for you to do your job and improve your school and community.

## Telling Your Story

Your community has a story to tell—a story of who you are, who your students are, and who the community is. Your story is one of challenges, but also of hope. The needs gaps in your community were created by any number of inequities and injustices, and when you identify these inequities and injustices, you can use them as talking points to get your students the things they need. Your story will help you to gain access to resources and funds that school budgets do not provide. If the person on the receiving end of your story is not supportive or does not understand why it is important to invest in your children, I suggest a blunt response: "If you do not invest in my children, they will rob your children." Sometimes you must be "real" with people for them to understand how serious the inequities are, and your story tells the truth—your students' truth.

Here are a couple of examples of stories I have used in the community-matching process:

> I serve the poorest congressional district in the United States. My school is surrounded by four housing projects that serve families who are living below the poverty level. The crime rate in the community is one of the highest in our city. The families are constantly complaining to me about

gun shooting and drug dealing in their buildings. The food options for the community are limited. Except for what is available at one super-market, most families do not have access to fresh produce, fish, and other healthy food options. There is no hospital in the area. Many of the families face health issues related to diabetes, asthma, and trauma. Most suffer from some form of mental health concern. Our families suffer from hunger anxiety and a lack of resources. These needs are the result of the conditions created by the inequities of the world in poverty. The reason I am asking you for support is because I have found it absolutely necessary to ask for funds to support our community garden so that we are able to provide our families with healthy food options.

Dear _____, I am writing you in reference to our music and arts program. Your organization is a staple in our community, and I know you donate funds to various schools for arts programs. Schools have received funds for instruments and teachers to support these programs. We would love to be included in this year's funding. As you know, we serve one of the poorest congressional districts in the United States. Many of our families struggle with finding money for food and other basic necessities. At our school, we do not have additional funds to pay for music and arts programs for our children. It is left to us to partner with organizations to provide these programs within our school. Our children will never have access to the arts unless we are able to provide it to them. As a school, we spend lots of funds on mental health supports for our families, and, sadly, we do not have funds for the arts. Please consider us in your future funding plans.

Here are a couple of examples of stories that offer a more personal perspective:

Growing up, I lived in a community like the one where I work. We did not have many programs in our community, and often we were left to figure out how to engage ourselves in activities. Sadly, some of my friends chose to get involved in illegal activity. I want the children I serve to have better options. I am asking for your support to provide our children with the kinds of programs and opportunities I did not have when I was growing up.

Growing up in a community where I had access to various enriching resources gave me insight into what resources I need to provide to the families I serve. I want our children to have a similar experience in life to the one I had growing up. I want our children to be able to participate in sports. When I was a kid, I was able to participate in sports programs in the community, and because of this exposure, I earned scholarships to attend various colleges. I want this opportunity to be afforded to the children I serve. If you fund our basketball program, we will be able to provide our children with a high-quality program enabling them to compete for scholarships like I did.

## Establishing Strategic Partnerships

To be successful as a community school, it is important to build relationships with partners who are actually going to help you achieve your vision and mission. Relationships are crucial for obtaining the resources we need, getting buy-in from the community, and securing advocates for the initiatives we want to implement.

Strategic partnerships can be seen as having a mutual benefit: the school benefits from the resources provided, and the partner gains visibility in the community and potential positive publicity. If you have a media relations office in your district, you can work with its staff to connect with local newspapers and other media outlets to inform the community about the partnership and its potential for positive impacts. Sometimes, in addition to positive publicity, partners are interested in gathering information about the community through surveys and other means. They likely are also interested in claiming a tax write-off, and you should be prepared to provide a letter confirming their donation.

Strategic partners often are not looking solely at the opportunity to benefit from a partnership, but also at ways to help the school or organization help students and their families. With this in mind, I make a point of not calling these partners "vendors," but instead refer to them as "partners" or "family." When you shift the way you talk about these partners and make them part of your school culture, they become vested in the work that you are doing in your school. At the end of the day, everything we do is about the children.

To develop strategic partnerships, you can begin by creating a list of people in your immediate circle—that is, people you can access right away, including family members, friends, and colleagues. You may be surprised by the people within your inner circle who can help you to gain access to the resources you want to secure. For example, when C.S. 55 was looking to partner with the fire department, I remembered that one of my high school friends, Miguel Flores, was an FDNY lieutenant. We had been out of touch after graduation, but we reconnected through social media. As two young Hispanic men from the Bronx, who would have known we would work together as professionals? Since reconnecting, we have collaborated on community events, and Miguel has provided resources for students on fire safety and taught them to know what a true medical emergency is and when to call 911. Similarly, my good friend Michelle Centeno, former president of the National Conference of Puerto Rican Women, helped me leverage my Puerto Rican heritage to gain resources for my school community. She provided scholarships to college-bound students, helped with food and clothing giveaways, and mentored me in my early years as a principal. She continues to support our efforts and frequently informs us about grant opportunities.

After identifying people in your inner circle, expand your list to include people in government, nonprofits, and other organizations. Doing this may require some legwork on your part. Attend community events and celebrations, and ask to be invited to community meetings as well. Getting resources is like playing the lottery: you must be in it to win it. If you do not put yourself out there, you are not going to be able to get the resources you need. Over time, you can establish a team of people who can do this work for you, but in the beginning, I highly recommend that you do it yourself. Potential donors always want to know that the head of the school is going to support the proposed project. Have business cards or another way of giving people your contact information so they can reach you at a later date. Branding your school with a logo that represents the work you are doing can help people easily identify you. Once you have potential donors' contact information, set up a meeting or invite them to visit your school or attend a special function. After you have established a relationship, most organizations require that you write a letter of interest to outline your proposal. Some may require a formal grant request with details on how you will use the funds.

When establishing partnerships and looking for resources, it is important to direct your effort toward the correct funding sources. Different kinds of projects and programs are funded through different categories of monies. For example, construction projects rely on capital funds. In New York City, these are called "Resolution A" funds, and they are distributed through grants from city council members and borough presidents. They can be used to build or upgrade spaces and to purchase technology. They cannot be used for something like establishing or expanding a music program. Funding for arts, music, and other programs comes through other sources, including noncapital funds distributed by elected officials and private organizations.

It is worth pointing out that enlisting elected officials as partners can be mutually beneficial. In fact, in my 30 years in education, I have found that one of the most important, if not *the* most important, relationships you have is that with your elected officials. You do not have to agree with everything they say or do, but one thing you have in common is that you want what is best for the families you serve. Elected officials view education as a priority, and it is important to them that the schools in their district be successful. Many constituents assess the effectiveness of an elected official by the quality of the schools and the surrounding community. Elected officials are often looking to partner with schools on community events, giveaways, and providing services to the families they serve.

At C.S. 55, we were able to secure more than $5 million in funding for capital projects, and through my work with former Bronx borough president Rubén Díaz Jr., we secured more than $30 million for schools across the Bronx. Díaz directly funded a $1 million schoolyard renovation at C.S. 55 and $300,000 in technology upgrades. In addition to the funds provided by Díaz, former city councilwoman Vanessa Gibson (now borough president of the Bronx) allocated $450,000 to a project to convert a space into a "caferary" (cafeteria/library) and helped us complete an $850,000 project to install air conditioning in the auditorium.

Elected officials may also fund arts programs. Through our partnership with the nonprofit organization Windows of Hip Hop and their CEO Melissa Libran, we are looking to open an $800,000 state-of-the-art music studio in the 2022–2023 school year, with funds jointly provided by Díaz and Gibson. Through Gibson and our partnership with the Bronx Children's Museum, we provide visual arts programs to our students. State senator Gustavo Rivera has funded hip hop classes, and former assemblyman Michael Blake and his predecessor, Chantel Jackson, have sponsored our step team and provided funds for musical instruments and tap dancing.

Be sure to check district policies before you contact an elected official for funds. Some may require that you get approval from your superintendent before doing so.

## Family Engagement

As you take on the job of creating a community school, keep in mind the importance of family engagement. I strongly believe that family engagement is the difference between a good school and a great school, and it is essential for actually accomplishing your goals. I tell people there is no such thing as "bad schools"; schools are just labeled that way because they serve the most challenging communities, and they are the hardest to get the best results from. What these schools also tend to have in common is poor family engagement. Greater family involvement in children's education leads to better student performance. It is common sense that children are more likely to reach their potential when they are given all the supports necessary for them to succeed—including from their families.

Family engagement is not just about bake sales; you should engage families in the school on various levels. Invite them to serve as mentors, tutors, classroom aides, home managers, translators, and other roles. Hold town hall meetings with the families and hear what they have to say. Send out surveys to get their input on the various initiatives you have in mind. Families must be part of school decision making. They should be active members of the parent-teacher associations, leadership teams, safety teams, and other decision-making groups. Engaging families as partners is a strategic move that will increase community morale. When families feel valued by the school or organization, they are more committed to its success. Keep in mind that when working with parents and caregivers, transparency is very important. Families need to know what is happening in the school building and how their children are being served. If you want community support, then involve the community in the school.

Districts across the United States have positions dedicated to supporting families. New York City, for example, has a family coordinator or parent coordinator position. This individual serves as the liaison between the school and families. Often when families have complaints or concerns, they turn to the family coordinator. The coordinator often provides workshops and other resources. If your district does not have such a position, you should identify someone in your school building who can serve in that capacity. This person can be an office aide, a secretary, or another staff member within the school whose primary responsibility is to support families. Having someone in this position who knows the community well, speaks multiple languages, and is resourceful is key to increasing family engagement.

## Next Up

The following chapters will illustrate how the community-school concept and the community-matching process work in addressing the six priorities: food, shelter, safety, health, access to technology, and education (specifically, considerations related to mental health, literacy, cultural relevance, and sports and arts programs). They can guide you as you begin the effort to extend your impact beyond the classroom by addressing the needs of students, their families, and the broader community population.

# Priority 1: Food

Do you find it hard to do your job or otherwise function when you're hungry? I know that I find it difficult to read and write when I'm hungry, and I'm pretty sure that when you're hungry you're not working at your best, either.

This observation applies to our children as well. We cannot expect them to do well in the classroom or to do homework when their stomachs are growling. Food has a major impact on student performance. If children are hungry, they won't be able to concentrate, and they may become agitated. Successfully educating them means that we must make sure that they are well fed, which is why I consider food to be the number-one priority.

The seriousness of the problem is evident when you look at how many children qualify for free or reduced-price lunch in the United States. In the 2015–2016 school year, nearly 27 million—more than 52 percent of all students—qualified (NCES, 2017). Qualification for free or reduced-price lunch is a measure that many districts use to determine the poverty level of the communities they serve. It is astonishing to find that in some communities, more than 98 percent of the children qualify. Their families are living below the poverty line and do not have access to enough food for their needs. It is outrageous that many of these communities—including the one we serve at C.S. 55—are in some of the richest cities in the world. Our families rely on food pantries, government assistance, and other ways of getting food for their children.

High-poverty communities not only have limited access to food; most of them also do not have access to healthy, high-quality food. Many are considered "food deserts." You can find a bodega or convenience store on every corner, but getting to the stores and supermarkets that offer more healthy food options requires people to travel long distances. Because many families do not have cars or have other challenges related to transportation, they often settle for whatever is nearby and affordable.

We know that many children are addicted to foods that are high in sugar, salt, and fat, as we see when they bring a soft drink and a bag of potato chips as a snack to school. Unfortunately, such foods are readily available at many convenience stores or bodegas, where the first thing you see when you walk in are sodas and other sugary drinks, along with unhealthy snacks. Often these foods cost less than healthy options, which is why most people who live in poverty choose them. These communities also typically have a variety of fast-food restaurants that offer relatively cheap but unhealthy food options, filled with sugar and salt, that contribute to health issues such as obesity and diabetes.

We know that access to healthy, high-quality food can contribute to children's success in school. But when educating families about the benefits of healthy eating, it is important to take into account cultural issues that can make it difficult to change their mindsets. For example, in my family, if you were thin, people thought you were sick, and they would look for ways to help you to gain weight. It was frowned upon to be lean. During family gatherings, if you were not "chubby" or what they thought was healthy, they would ask your parents: "Is he sick? Is he not eating well?" To help you gain weight, the family would give you food loaded with sugar and fat. Your morning coffee had milk and spoons of added sugar. Meals often included sugary drinks, and we were taught that "soda tastes good with everything." When I was a child, it was cheaper for me to buy a 25-cent "juice" drink filled with sugar than a bottle of water.

Aside from the sugary drinks, we also ingested plenty of unhealthy foods that were part of Puerto Rican culture, including roasted pork, pepper steak, white rice, and fried foods. Even if traditional foods include some healthy ingredients, they may also include the highly processed products that are so common in the United States, with high levels of sugar and salt. Avoiding such ingredients allows traditional meals to be both tasty and nutritious.

The point is that even when families have access to food, the food is not necessarily healthy. "Having some food is better than having no food," someone once told me. That is true, but as school and community leaders, we must ensure that no child ever goes hungry *and* that the foods they are eating are healthy.

When we began the community-matching process for the food priority at C.S. 55, we found that access to healthy food was a major need for our community, and although options for buying food were available, most of them were inadequate. Fast-food restaurants and bodegas were everywhere, but there were no fruit-and-vegetable stands. To address this problem, we needed to look for various partners within the community. We crafted a story to tell organizations about our school. The fact that many of our children lived in poverty and lacked healthy food options made it easy to request help. Knowing specifically what we needed enabled us to get support for various projects, including establishing a garden (which we call a "farm") at the school to grow our own healthy food and getting local restaurants to provide our families with cooked meals.

What we were able to accomplish at C.S. 55 illustrates how the community-matching process can lead to significant improvements for a school and the families it serves. The next sections describe how you can use the community-matching process to tackle the number-one priority: food.

## Identifying the Gaps

A good way to begin identifying the gaps between food needs and availability is to arrange a community walk with the constituents of your school or organization. This group can consist of parents, teachers, staff, students, community leaders, and others who will walk with you to identify food sources in the neighborhood. Look for bodegas or small grocery stores, supermarkets, restaurants, food pantries, and other organizations that could possibly provide resources. Start to identify the key people in each of the establishments that you could connect with. Also look for ways that these organizations can help to promote the healthy-food options you want for your community. For example, when you enter a bodega, is soda the first thing you see? If so, does the store also sell healthier items such as fruit juices or dairy products that could be displayed more prominently? Do the restaurants offer healthy menu choices? Do the community-based organizations have health initiatives that you can join? Are there resources you could bring into your school or organization?

Here are some questions to ask when evaluating the food needs of your students and community and identifying the gaps:

- What are the food-related needs of your school community?
- Where do the families in your community get most of their food (grocery stores, bodegas, convenience stores, supermarkets, fast-food restaurants, etc.)? You can distribute a confidential survey to families to collect this information.

- Are healthy food options available in your community? If so, are they affordable?

- How many of your students qualify for free or reduced-price lunch?

- Are there food pantries in the neighborhood?

- What are the food resources your school offers to the community (free or reduced-price lunch, food giveaways, etc.)?

- Does the school have space for a food pantry?

- How does not having food or healthy food options affect your students and the community?

- What percentage of people in the community have diabetes? How does this compare with state and national averages?

## Specifying Needs

As discussed in Chapter 1, understanding the difference between needs and wants is important in specifying what you will be requesting. You may *want* something, but it might not be necessary to have it immediately—or to have it at all, if it is not something that will help you to improve families' access to basic resources. Needs should always be your priority.

Here are some questions to ask to help you specify your needs:

- What percentage of students at your school qualify for free or reduced-price lunch?

- Are students coming to the school hungry?

- Do students have access to healthy food?

- Do you need to provide food to positively affect students' quality of life?

- Is diabetes a problem in your school community?

- Do you have space to create a community garden?

- Do you need a food pantry?

- Are there restaurants in the community to partner with?
- Does your school have a cooking program?

## Telling Your Story

When you visit the organizations whose support you are seeking, it is important to have your school's story clearly defined, with your needs transparent. Here is an example:

> More than 90 percent of our students qualify for free or reduced-price lunch. This means that most of our families live below the poverty level, with an annual income of less than $30,000, in New York City. We want to provide food to our families through our food pantries, and we need your support. If you provide $2,000 worth of food monthly, we can achieve the goal of feeding these families.

Here are some questions to ask as you craft your story:

- What are the demographics of your school community (race, ethnicity, socioeconomic status, etc.)?
- How can you quantify the lack of available food (lack of grocery stores, distance to grocery stores, etc.)?
- How can you quantify the excessive cost of food?
- What is the nutritional value of easily available food?
- What is it, specifically, that you are asking for? (For example, are you requesting a specific amount of money per month to supply a food pantry?)
- What is your organization's mission?
- Why is access to food and healthy eating important for your students?
- What health issues exist in the community due to lack of food options?
- How does food (e.g., hunger, unhealthy snacks) affect student performance?
- How will improved access to healthy food support your school mission and vision?

## Establishing Strategic Partnerships

Finding partners to address the food priority involves reaching out to local restaurants, stores, food pantries, and other organizations that can support your efforts. Here are action steps to take:

- Make a list of all the people you think can help.
- Do research online to find organizations that address hunger and donate food to the community.
- Contact the community-based organizations you want to partner with.
- Visit organizations that you believe will help address the priority of food.
- Invite partners to visit your school and discuss what your plans are for addressing this priority.
- Meet with community leaders and elected officials to discuss possible solutions.

Here are some questions to ask as you consider possible partnerships:

- Does the organization have a history of donating food and resources?
- Do the products it provides meet the needs of the community? That is, does the community eat the foods being donated?
- What is the organization willing to commit to? Is it going to be a one-time donation or a long-term partnership?
- Where is the partner organization located? Is it easily accessible for many of your families?
- How can the partner support your efforts?
- Why do you think the partner is a good fit for your organization?

## A Community-Matching Worksheet for the Food Priority

Completing the worksheet introduced in Chapter 1 can help you organize and record your community-matching efforts for the food priority. The worksheet has spaces for each part of the process: identifying the gaps between needs and available resources, specifying needs, telling your story, and establishing strategic partnerships. Figure 2.1 is an example of a completed worksheet for the food priority.

## FIGURE 2.1

---

## Sample Community-Matching Worksheet for Priority 1: Food

### Identifying the Gaps

Through our community-matching process, we found that the school needs to provide food support for families. Many of our families live below the poverty line, and the school currently does not have any resources aside from the regular school meals provided to the children daily. The surrounding community has a supermarket, two bodegas (small grocery stores), and a few fast-food restaurants. The school is in the middle of a food desert. Our children have a hard time focusing because they are either hungry or eating unhealthy food. Many of the food pantries are limited in the amount of food they can provide. Most shelters do not allow families to cook food in their facilities.

### Specifying Needs

The community needs support to provide families with better access to healthy food options. The school needs to establish partnerships with the local food sources (bodegas, supermarket, pantries, and restaurants). If space permits, a food pantry needs to be established in the school. Healthy snacks can be provided to the students daily. Workshops and classes on healthy eating can be offered to the families. A community garden can be created to grow healthy produce. The school needs funds to open and maintain the food pantry and also to pay for extra meals.

### Telling Your Story

We serve the poorest congressional district in the United States. Many of our families live below the poverty level. Our children do not have access to healthy and consistent meals, and families depend on the school for their essentials. The children suffer from hunger and, as a result, have difficulty focusing on learning. The unhealthy food options in the community have led to a high rate of obesity, which in turn has led to an increasing number of children and family members suffering from diabetes. We need healthy food options for our families, and we need to work with the community to increase the availability of food. If you provide us with a monthly budget of $3,000 and connect us with the local food distribution center, we will be

*continued*

**FIGURE 2.1** (*continued*)

---

**Sample Community-Matching**
**Worksheet for Priority 1: Food**

able to provide food to our families through our pantry and even offer food on the weekends. We are willing to provide you with the space to make this initiative possible.

**Establishing Strategic Partnerships**
Bodegas can work on providing healthy foods at a reduced price. Restaurants can offer free food or food at reduced prices to families at the end of the day, when most restaurants throw food away. Most community centers have kitchens that can be made available for families who are living in shelters. Often food is donated to shelters, but the residents need a place to cook their meals. The success of elected officials is based on their ability to provide resources to their communities, and in high-poverty neighborhoods, food pantries are among the most important resources. Sports organizations, nonprofits, and other organizations generally have a community relations office or staff member whose responsibilities may include working to address the inequities of the community, including access to healthy food.

## What We Learned from the Pandemic

The pandemic revealed how serious a problem food insecurity is in the United States. As a nation, we came to realize that literally millions of families rely on schools to feed their children—for example, through the free and reduced-price lunch program. At C.S. 55, we were able to help sustain our families during the pandemic-related school closures through the partnerships we had established with various food pantries and other providers.

# Sample Projects

Healthy-food initiatives come in many forms. The following are descriptions of some sample projects to address the food priority. They may give you ideas for how you can address this issue at your school.

## Partnerships with Restaurants

My good friend Junior Martinez is president of the Hoodspitality Group, whose mission is to build community-based restaurants and other businesses. This organization operates according to the belief that communities and small-business owners should work collaboratively for the true advancement of a neighborhood. They are constantly looking to build relationships with community leaders, educators, and nonprofit organizations, and to create platforms to provide necessary resources to the most vulnerable families. Events they have sponsored include an annual back-to-school backpack giveaway and block party, turkey giveaways at Thanksgiving, and holiday toy drives. In a recent initiative called "Feeding the First Responders," they provided 25,000 free meals to local workers from the community. This initiative caught the attention of multiple nonprofit organizations and governmental agencies that later joined us to cook, prep, and deliver one million meals to date to the most food-insecure residents in the Bronx.

## Celebrations and Parties

School celebrations and parent-engagement meetings can be opportunities to make food available to the community. If you advertise that "food will be served" during these events, you can expect a high turnout. After you do some research on costs and delivery methods, you can approach partners with a specific request for funding. Potential partners may include elected officials and other community leaders, health insurers and care providers, supermarkets, and restaurants. Many restaurants will provide free food to the community as a way of giving back, clearing their inventory, and securing a tax write-off. Pizza parties are popular, but pizza can be unhealthy, so consider also featuring smoothies, fruit salad, and other nutritious options at some of these events.

## In-School Food Pantries

If your school has space for a food pantry and you decide to host one, be strategic about the foods you fill it with. Do not overstock it with sugary drinks and unhealthy snacks. I understand that sometimes these are the items that are donated, but you must remind your partners to provide healthy foods. Elected officials, community-based organizations, and community leaders are often willing to support food pantries. You can also form a team to write a grant proposal for government funds.

Keep in mind that the "pantry" concept can be used to distribute things other than food, as at C.S. 55's Tiger Bodega, which provides clothing and backpacks as well as food. Through a partnership with an organization called Soles4Souls, C.S. 55 was able to give away more than 700 pairs of sneakers. In addition, through another partnership with the nonprofit organization New York Cares, we gave away 400 coats.

## Community Gardens

Many schools have community gardens. At C.S. 55, our "farm" provides organic produce for the community, including cancer patients, who particularly benefit from the absence of chemical additives in their food. School gardens can be located outdoors, using raised beds or planter boxes, or they can use indoor technology, such as aeroponic gardening, which allows plants to be grown without soil. Information on developing a school garden—including finding the necessary space, safety issues, providing food for the school cafeteria, funding, and other topics—is available from the Office of Community Food Systems of the U.S. Department of Agriculture (https://fns-prod.azureedge.us/sites/default/files/resource-files/USDA_OCFS_FactSheet_SchoolGardens_508.pdf). Funding may come from government agencies, community-based organizations, and community leaders. At C.S. 55, we were able to secure funds for our farm from the American Diabetes Foundation and Montefiore Hospital and through our partnership with a nonprofit organization called the Green Bronx Machine (see Chapter 5 for more information on our partnership with the Green Bronx Machine).

### Cooking Programs

Providing a cooking program in the school can be a fun and engaging way to teach children about how the foods they eat affect them both physically and mentally, including their ability to learn and grow. You can expand the program into a community-education effort by inviting students' families to participate. At C.S. 55, our families learn how to grow their own food and how to prepare meals that are both tasty and nutritious. We've been able to secure funding through elected officials who are interested in demonstrating their support for improving the health of the communities they serve. We even received funding from the New York Yankees baseball team, which is based in the Bronx.

## The Bottom Line

Food is priority number one for good reason. We know that hunger leads to many mental and physical health issues. It can affect children's ability to focus and perform to their potential, and it also has an impact on student attendance. Believe it or not, violence and crime can be correlated to people being hungry and not having access to food (Caughron, 2016). Addressing the food priority must be at the top of the list in our efforts to support our children and families.

# Priority 2: Shelter

Shelter is a priority that I rank second only to food in its importance for ensuring the well-being of our children. No child should ever worry about where they are going to be sleeping at night. We are failing as a society if we do not fix the housing situation in the United States. A 2020 report on homelessness from the U.S. Department of Housing and Urban Development provides statistics from a single night in January when a count was conducted (Henry, de Sousa, Roddey, Gayen, & Bednar, 2021). It showed that nearly 600,000 people were homeless on that date, including more than 170,000 families with children. Further, homelessness affected Black and Brown people in disproportionate numbers. According to the Coalition for the Homeless (2022), a social services organization in New York City, more than 10,000 families sleep in shelters throughout the city on any given night; during the course of 2021, nearly 32,000 homeless children in New York

City slept in a shelter. Children staying in shelters often have to deal with safety issues as well as uncomfortable living situations. They may not get enough sleep or have adequate resources, including internet access, to do their homework.

In addition to those who are homeless, many children whose families are below the poverty line live in some form of temporary housing, or they live "doubled up" with relatives in conditions that are inconvenient or unsafe. Having to share only one shower or bathroom with many other people can lead to students being late to school and to cleanliness issues. Far too many apartments are infested with rats and roaches; building elevators may not work; and dangers such as the presence of lead paint are all too common.

These and other safety issues—including crime—are a major concern. My father was the superintendent of two buildings in the Bronx during the 1970s and '80s. He ran those buildings with high standards and fought to keep the drugs out, believing that if you raise the standards of the community, the poor conditions will improve.

Having seen firsthand the work of my father within our community, I came to believe that if we work closely with our communities, if we invest in our communities, we can change the outcome for our children. Community schools and organizations must work hard to raise standards related to safe and secure housing. The hope is that by raising these standards, we will positively affect the living conditions of our children.

We can begin by becoming aware of the specific housing situations that our families face (as outlined in the Identifying the Gaps section that follows). Then, we must have people in our schools who can assist our families with housing. Often we find that parents do not fill out applications for permanent housing due to language issues or an inability to read. Handling this critical communication issue is just one reason why it is so important that we establish support services within our schools where parents can go for help.

## Identifying the Gaps

As I suggested for the food priority discussed in Chapter 2, a community walk is a good way to identify the gaps between housing needs and housing availability. As part of the community-matching process, C.S. 55 conducted a community walk to find out about our students' housing situation. We found that most of our families were living in housing projects for low-income families or in "doubled-up" apartments. The inadequacies of these options are apparent for all the reasons mentioned earlier, including overcrowding, insect and rodent infestation, unhealthy indoor and outdoor environments, and crime. We also found that there were no partners in the school working with the housing or shelter issues that our community is facing.

As bad as many of these housing options are, at least they provide children with a place to live. Some children come to our schools every day—including to C.S. 55—not knowing where they will be the next day. Their parents or caregivers may have been told by a shelter employee that they must leave the premises at 8:00 a.m. and find another place to spend the night. It is no wonder that the families of these children make housing a priority over education.

As educators in community schools working with challenging communities, we must find ways to support our families as they deal with housing. At C.S. 55, we realized that a significant gap in addressing the issue was the fact that there was no one at the school who had the knowledge or background to provide support or act as a liaison. We recognized the need to employ a person or an organization to provide this service, as either their primary or one of their primary responsibilities. Family liaisons, social workers, or parent coordinators can be recruited for this position. Schools can establish "family centers" where people can go to get information related to housing. At C.S. 55, we partnered with a nonprofit organization called Graham Windham that provides services to children and families in New York City.

As you are identifying the gaps and evaluating the housing needs of your students and community, here are some questions to ask:

- What are the needs of your school community related to housing?
- What are the resources your school offers to the community?
- What resources does the surrounding community have to offer?
- How do the living conditions of the families affect your students and the community?
- How many families live in shelters?
- What percentage of the families you serve are homeless?
- Are there community-based programs that provide housing-related services?

## Specifying Needs

When it comes to housing, it is likely that whatever your school is looking to provide will be a *need*, not a *want*. Decent housing is an essential right and is directly related to students' attendance at school, as well as their performance.

Knowing how important housing is to your students' well-being, it is critical that you identify a person or a team of people who can support your families in their search for a safe and stable place to live. As mentioned earlier, often families are unable to find the appropriate housing or shelter situation because of language barriers or illiteracy; many struggle to find the time to look for resources. Having someone in the school who is an expert in the field—or who can learn and share vital information about processes and options—can have a major impact on your ability to properly serve your community.

Many schools in New York City have a position called the parent coordinator. This is a staff member who has been assigned to support families by finding resources, addressing parent concerns, and responding to complaints. This person is an advocate for parents within the school. If you do not have funding to create such a position, you might want to see if you can get a parent volunteer or someone who has knowledge of the community to fill this role. The person in this role needs to do outreach to various organizations within the community, build relationships with the families, and work closely with the school staff. If possible, you can create a welcome center in the school that is maintained by the staff member or parent volunteer—a place where families can come and ask questions and get the resources they need.

As you determine needs related to the housing priority, you can ask the following questions:

- Is housing an area of concern in your community?
- Are language barriers or literacy issues a problem for families in communicating with housing authorities?
- Does the school require a housing coordinator?
- Do you need to partner with a program that focuses on the housing issues in your community?

## Telling Your Story

As with the food priority, when you visit the organizations whose support you are seeking to address your community's housing needs, it is important to have your school's story clearly defined, with your needs transparent. Here is an example of a story to address the housing priority:

> Our families live below the poverty line. Because they cannot afford adequate housing, many of them are forced to live in shelters and other forms of temporary housing. Many of our families have children who are unable to focus on their academics because of the various issues that exist in their homes. I am reaching out to your organization for support in providing workshops and staff who would be willing to support our parents in requesting permanent housing. I know firsthand the impact that poor living conditions have on our children, for many of my friends live in similar conditions. No child should ever be worried about where they will be sleeping at night, and no family should have to struggle to provide a home for their children.

Here are questions to ask as you craft your story:

- What are the demographics of your school community (race, ethnicity, socioeconomic status, etc.)?
- How many families live in temporary housing?
- Why is housing important to your families?
- Can you think of a time when something related to housing had a negative impact on a student?
- How do the living conditions of the children at your school affect their academic performance? How do the conditions affect their behavior?

## Establishing Strategic Partnerships

Schools in high-poverty areas must establish partnerships with the local shelters and housing facilities or projects. At C.S. 55, as we identified the gaps in our students' housing situations, we also discovered contacts and resources. We learned that the various housing facilities had their own managers. We were able to identify the directors of the shelters in the school neighborhood. These individuals served as social workers and were able to provide assistance to families looking for permanent housing. We also identified tenant association presidents who could provide support. In addition, we found that staff members working for elected officials were available to help families in completing applications for housing and in reporting leaks and other issues tenants often must deal with. We also identified nonprofit organizations that could provide access to necessary resources.

You may find many of these same resources in your community. If your families cannot advocate for themselves, for whatever reason, you must establish ties with as many helpful partners as possible to ensure that your families have adequate living facilities.

Here are some questions to ask as you look for partners to address the housing priority:

- Do you know anyone who works in the area of concern? If so, make a list of all the people you think can help.

- What organizations do you know of that work to address housing issues? Whom could you ask to help you conduct research on possible partners?

- Who are the presidents of the local shelters and tenant associations? What is their contact information?

- Who are your local elected officials? Invite them to your school.

- What, specifically, are potential partners willing to do to help?

- Do the partners provide funding or access to housing?

- What does the partner need from you to support your efforts?

## A Community-Matching Worksheet for the Shelter Priority

Completing the worksheet introduced in Chapter 1 can help you organize and record your community-matching efforts for the shelter priority. The worksheet has spaces for each part of the process: identifying the gaps between needs and available resources, specifying needs, telling your story, and establishing strategic partnerships. Figure 3.1 is an example of a completed worksheet for the shelter priority.

### FIGURE 3.1

---

### Sample Community-Matching Worksheet for Priority 2: Shelter

#### Identifying the Gaps
Through our community-matching process, we found that many of our families live in various forms of temporary housing. Some of them live in shelters, and some are doubled up in apartments until they can find their own living space. Others live in housing projects. Our school does not have anyone in the building whose job it is to address issues related to housing, including maintaining contacts with homeless shelters. We have no accurate way to actually know who is homeless or not.

#### Specifying Needs
Our homeless families are faced with having to find somewhere to sleep every night. They need help finding a stable, affordable place to live.

Children who are living in a place that is clean and safe are more likely to be successful in school. Our school needs someone who can monitor the housing situation of our students. We need to identify a staff member or parent volunteer who could work closely with families to gather relevant information and to act as a liaison between the school and various housing organizations to ensure that the housing needs of all families are being met. Our school needs an office or other space where families can go to get information, answers to their questions, and other support.

### Telling Your Story

Many of our children cannot focus on their education because they do not have a stable living situation. Their families must look for places to sleep every night. If these children had permanent housing, their attendance rate would increase, and they would have one less concern to distract them from classroom activities. I am reaching out to see if you can support us in our efforts to provide information to help our families address their housing needs and to work with local housing organizations. We would like to have a staff member who could act as a liaison to support our families. Currently, we do not have the funds to hire a housing liaison. We are asking for funds to create this position and to establish an office or other space in the school that would be used by families as a resource to get advice and information about housing. We are also asking to partner with your office to provide some of these supports directly through your organization.

### Establishing Strategic Partnerships

Local elected officials have liaisons within their offices who are responsible for housing and shelters. We need to work with them to ensure we have adequate resources to help our families deal with housing issues. Potential partners also include social workers who could provide individual and whole-family support. Many housing organizations have offices and staff who are available to provide advice and information. The staff at local shelters can also be helpful. Communicating with them about the importance of ensuring that families have internet access and cooking facilities can improve our families' experience in these temporary housing situations.

### What We Learned from the Pandemic

COVID-19 exposed the fact that poor living conditions were part of the problem that led to widespread infections among many of our Black and Brown families. Poorly maintained homes and apartments, with—among other things—inadequate ventilation and dangers such as lead paint, had already led to many of our children having underlying health conditions, such as asthma, which made them more vulnerable to the virus. Even in non-pandemic circumstances, we know that trash should not be left around living areas, and that playgrounds and common spaces in the school and surrounding community must be cleaned and maintained regularly. The pandemic brought additional requirements for regular disinfection of building entrances and other spaces.

Overcrowded living conditions made it difficult for many children to find the space to do school assignments at home or to sign on to virtual education platforms for online classes. Continual distractions and noise often added to the challenges, and many children fell far behind.

The pandemic shone a bright light on the glaring inequities in housing that characterize many of our communities. It reminded us of the need to do all we can to address the issue.

## Sample Projects

Here are descriptions of sample projects that address issues related to housing. They may give you ideas for how your school can work on this priority.

### Housing Coordinator

Every community school should have someone who can address issues related to housing. You must identify someone who can support families and build relationships with supervisors of the various housing organizations. The person should be familiar with application processes and the rules that govern homeless shelters and other housing facilities. If you cannot afford to have a staff member take on this responsibility, you may be able to find a volunteer or have the parent coordinator support this effort.

## Monthly Meetings with the Housing Authority and Elected Officials

Schedule monthly online meetings with the elected officials in your community to discuss your concerns. Doing so creates a transparent process of accountability and supports the needs of families. This is also an opportunity to get answers to your questions about housing.

## Community Walks

A monthly walk around the community is a good way to see first-hand the kinds of housing families are living in and the overall conditions of the neighborhood. Such walks also provide an opportunity to locate housing organizations and other potential partners. A group of staff members and parents can take part in these walks and share their observations.

## Complaint and Concern Box

A box located in the school's main office can provide a convenient place for families to deposit complaints and concerns related to housing. A staff member should gather the submissions and forward them to local elected officials, tenant association presidents, and other people who can act on the information provided.

## Community Clean-Up

In partnership with local elected officials, students and community members can be paid a stipend to help keep the community clean. This will engage the youth to reduce the violence and crime in the community while maintaining the environment.

## The Bottom Line

Schools can have a positive impact on children's day-to-day living environments—and their performance and behavior in school—by addressing the housing situation in the community. Something as simple as the ability to get a good night's sleep can make a big difference, as we know that sleep deprivation leads to a lack of focus, with negative consequences in the classroom. The more we assist our families with the basic human need for decent housing, the greater the impact we will have on the lives of our children.

# Priority 3: Safety

Through a good friend of mine—author, sports commentator, and New York Yankees executive Ray Negron—I once invited Hank Steinbrenner to C.S. 55. Hank Steinbrenner was the son of George Steinbrenner, former owner of the Yankees. We brought him into the school to see how we could get him to fund some of the school's programs. As we walked around the building, we stepped into a preK classroom where people had complained of being too cold. When we looked around the room, we found bullet holes in the window. The cold air was coming through the holes. The preK class had not been in session the day before, when the incident apparently took place. Had the children been in the classroom, who knows what would have happened? I looked over at Hank Steinbrenner and noticed that his eyes were tearing up. He looked at me and asked, "What do you need for your school?" At that moment, he realized that the conditions our children and families live under are dangerous, and their struggle is real.

Hank Steinbrenner died in 2020, but Ray Negron continues to come to the school to donate holiday gifts, even bringing along Yankees players to autograph items for the children. The Yankees organization has also helped to fund arts and other programs at C.S. 55.

Sometimes we need to make things "real" to get people to understand why safety is an ongoing concern in many school communities. It is sad that the world is so beautiful in so many ways, yet a horrific thing like bullet holes in a preK classroom window reminds us of another side of life.

## Identifying the Gaps

Children need to feel safe to be able to focus in the classroom, and an important first step in ensuring their safety is to identify the gaps between the resources the school currently has and the resources it needs. These resources may include safety policies and procedures; equipment, such as security cameras; and personnel, such as a school safety team (these and other measures are described in the Sample Projects section of this chapter).

Here are some questions to ask when identifying the gaps in the resources your school provides to address the safety needs of your students and community:

- What are the needs of your school community in terms of safety?
- What are the safety-related resources your school offers to the community?
- What resources does the surrounding community have to offer?
- Does the school have security cameras?
- Does the school have an active safety team?
- Is the school located in a high-crime community?

Sometimes we find that the safety priority intersects with other priorities, such as shelter, and we discover a gap that should be addressed. For example, one of the worst fires in New York City history occurred recently in the Bronx, where the lack of heat in an apartment building forced families to use space heaters. A malfunctioning space heater resulted in an electrical fire that killed 18 people, including two former C.S. 55 students and several relatives of one of my staff members. As a school leader, I believe that we could have done more to support the families and prevent the fire by, for example, offering workshops on fire safety.

## Specifying Needs

The critical need to ensure safety is obvious when we consider the fact that we might reasonably assume all the children and youth in many communities suffer from some form of post-traumatic stress disorder, or PTSD. In fact, the term *post*-traumatic may not be accurate, because the condition is ongoing.

A simple test to see the impact of trauma on our children involves asking them to close their eyes for three minutes. I often do this when the students are gathered in the auditorium, and when I observe how they respond, I find that most of them cannot keep their eyes closed. When I have asked the children why they can't close their eyes, they often say they don't feel safe. Even in a school building that has security cameras, security agents, and many caring adults, the children still have issues with safety.

Here are some questions to ask to help you identify the gaps in what your school provides to address the safety priority:

- Do you need cameras in the school?
- Are the police involved in your school at a level that is appropriate to the needs for safety and security?
- What is the crime rate in the community?
- Do you need a safety team? If so, whom could you recruit to be part of the team?
- Do you have a dean or an administrator in charge of safety?

## Telling Your Story

When you visit the organizations that might support your efforts related to safety, you should have your story clearly defined, with your needs transparent. Here is an example:

> We serve a community with one of the highest crime rates in the city. The children are constantly exposed to gangs, violence, and other unsafe situations. With your support, we can create a safe environment where the children and families can come to escape the dangers they face regularly. Having cameras throughout the school and around the perimeter of the school will help us to secure our building. It would cost $93,000 to complete this project and install all the equipment necessary.

Here are some questions to ask as you work on crafting your story:

- What are the demographics of your school community (race, ethnicity, socioeconomic status, etc.)?
- What is the crime rate in the community?
- Why is it important to create a safe environment in the school?
- Was there a specific incident in the community that caused children to feel unsafe?
- Has anything happened in the school that requires you to focus on safety?
- How will improving the safety of the children and community affect student performance?

## Establishing Strategic Partnerships

The work of creating a safe environment cannot stop at the school door. As educators in community schools, we must leverage our partners to provide social and emotional support for our children. It is important that we establish ties with the police and fire departments, elected officials, community leaders, and staff members of various social service agencies that can provide support to the families we serve. You can also do research online to find nonprofit organizations that provide funding and guidance in this priority area. Finally, you can hold in-person or virtual meetings with community leaders and elected officials to discuss possible solutions.

Here are action items to consider as you begin the work of developing strategic partnerships related to safety:

- Make a list of all the people you think can help.
- Research organizations that work to address safety issues.
- Contact the fire and police departments about support they could provide.
- Partner with elected officials.
- Schedule a meeting with the safety director in your school district.

    Here are questions to ask:

- What are the one or two most important safety issues your school is facing?
- What kind of organization is in the best position to help you address these safety issues?
- Who are the key individuals in the community who could support your safety efforts?
- Are there district or government funds that could support safety improvements in your school?

## A Community-Matching Worksheet for the Safety Priority

Completing the worksheet introduced in Chapter 1 can help you organize and record your community-matching efforts for the safety priority. The worksheet has spaces for each part of the process: identifying the gaps between needs and available resources, specifying needs, telling your story, and establishing strategic partnerships. Figure 4.1 is an example of a completed worksheet for the safety priority.

## FIGURE 4.1

### Sample Community-Matching Worksheet for Priority 3: Safety

#### Identifying the Gaps

Through our community-matching process, we found that the school lacks sufficient safety support for our families. The community has a high crime rate, and creating a school environment where the children feel safe must be a priority. Many of our children complain that they cannot focus because of shootings and other violence in the community. Currently we do not have all the equipment we need to create the safest possible school environment, or strong partnerships with organizations that could help us address families' concerns about violence and safety. We also do not have a safe community space within the school where families can get information and resources to support them. This space would provide a place where members of the community could come to escape the challenges they face daily. We would like to set up a room for them to be able to get coffee, sit comfortably, and use a computer without feeling concern for their safety. If available, a social worker can manage the space and provide services.

#### Specifying Needs

The school needs security cameras to ensure the safety of our children and staff. The cameras would be placed outside around the school perimeter and throughout the school building. We also need a video station near the security desk and the principal's office. In addition, we need to establish a relationship with the local police and elected officials to provide the families with daily supports. There needs to be a liaison who can work to build relationships among the police, elected officials, and the community. The local police precinct can create a community room where families can get necessary information and support. Monthly meetings can be scheduled to air the concerns of the community.

#### Telling Your Story

We serve a community that has one of highest crime rates in New York City. Our children face trauma daily, and they look to the school for safety. To keep our children and staff safe, we need security cameras in and around the school building. If you help us to purchase and install such cameras, we believe our students would feel less stressed and would be able to focus on their learning. The cameras would also deter people from committing crimes on school property. Sadly, we do not have the $30,000 we estimate is necessary for us to purchase the 10 cameras and the security station necessary to cover our complex. Thus, we are reaching out to you for your support. Our children deserve to attend a school that is safe and nurturing for all.

**Establishing Strategic Partnerships**

Elected officials have control over grants and other ways of providing funding for cameras and other security devices. Safety is always a top priority on their agenda, and they are good potential partners for getting the resources we need to create a safe learning environment for our children. In New York City, the Department of Education has officials responsible for helping schools ensure the safety of our children and community. We also need to involve the police and fire departments in our plans to create safe spaces. Finally, federal and state agencies offer grants to fund the purchase of cameras and other safety equipment.

## What We Learned from the Pandemic

During the pandemic, we found out that schools and communities could be doing more to keep children safe—not only from physical danger but also from the threat of infectious disease. Further, adults need to be kept safe as well. Like schools throughout the United States and the rest of the world, C.S. 55 struggled to remain open during the early phase of the pandemic. After reopening, we had to change many of our normal procedures. We all had to learn how to keep a safe distance from each other, wear masks, and wash hands appropriately. The whole structure of the school environment had to change to meet the conditions of the pandemic. Class sizes were reduced, and large gatherings were no longer allowed. We had to conduct regular temperature checks to ensure that no one had a fever— a symptom that could indicate a COVID infection. Even after the school reopened, some staff and students (for example, those with underlying conditions that placed them at higher risk for severe illness) remained at home and had to adapt to teaching and learning full-time in a virtual environment. These new procedures affected many of our families, but they were necessary to keep everyone safe.

Virtual learning was a major struggle for schools and families—especially for those whose caregivers were unable to work from home. Not all working parents and guardians had the ability to stay home with their children on the days they were scheduled for virtual learning. Schools had to establish partnerships and figure out how to provide services to students on their virtual days without negatively impacting families. To accommodate as many in-person learners as possible as safely as possible, schools needed to maximize their space. Increasing the number of instructional spaces meant hiring additional staff, however, which was a challenge. To get through this tough time safely at C.S. 55, our only option was to hire less-qualified staff at a lower pay scale. It was not an ideal situation, but it was what we had to do to survive during this period.

From a safety perspective, the pandemic was a nightmare for schools in low-income neighborhoods: many parents and caregivers had no choice but to send their children to schools that were not adequately equipped to cope with COVID. More than ever before, it became apparent that schools must partner with community-based organizations to augment childcare while parents work, providing safe, high-quality support for any children who need it.

# Sample Projects

Here are descriptions of sample projects that address issues related to safety. They may give you ideas for how your school can work on this priority.

### Security Cameras

Working with the borough safety administrator and local elected officials, C.S. 55 was able to secure funds to purchase security cameras and install them throughout the building. The cameras provide video footage of activity at the school's various entries and exits as well as throughout the hallways.

### Police as Partners

The police must be partners in creating a safe environment, especially during this time when many communities are dealing with important questions about how the police engage with citizens. The police can support community events, movie nights, and other ways of engaging community members in a positive way. Most police departments have a community relations office or team that you can work with. The police do not necessarily have funds to invest in schools, but they do have resources and can be partners in addressing safety needs within the community—for example, through cameras and Safe Streets initiatives. The police can also support the safety of the teachers and staff by patrolling parking areas and the perimeter of school and creating safe passages for the children. Inviting representatives of the police to parent meetings and staff meetings is a good way for them to engage in conversations with your school community. The more you develop a relationship between the police and the community, the easier it is for law enforcement to provide a safe environment for your families. Finally, invite police officers to career day at your school. Take advantage of any opportunities for them to engage with the children and increase the likelihood that children's perceptions will be positive.

## School Safety Team

Every community school should have a safety team. In New York City, it is required by law. The safety team should consist of parents, students, school staff, and, depending on the personnel available at your school, people such as school-safety agents and health and wellness support staff. The safety team will be responsible for putting together a safety plan to guide all aspects of safety and preparedness for the school. If your school has a building-response team, the safety team can also collaborate with them to coordinate safety drills. The administration should be informed by the recommendations of the school safety team, which can serve as a channel for staff members, parents, and children to voice their concerns and complaints, as well as their satisfaction, regarding safety and readiness.

The safety team could also serve as a liaison with local elected officials and representatives of the fire and police departments.

Regular meetings and community forums can be organized jointly to address the safety needs of the community. Ongoing communication with local elected officials and the police department around safety can help to reassure people that their concerns are being heard.

Community members should also receive updates on gang activity and other violence happening in the area and what is being done to address these dangers. Often these safety issues outside the school find their way into the school building. They can affect student attendance and children's mental health. Higher crime rates correlate with increases in childhood trauma, which in turn affects students' ability to be successful in school. In order to successfully educate our children, we must ensure that their mental health needs are being satisfied. (See Chapter 7 for more on mental health issues.)

## Town Halls Focused on Public Safety

Monthly meetings can be scheduled with the local police precincts, elected officials, and community leaders. This will be a collaboration between the school community and the police officers serving them. It also allows for updates and analysis of data. The more you increase the transparency by the police with the community, the greater the trust will be between them.

## Police Cadet Program

Reach out to your local police precinct to see if they offer a cadet program. When families view the police as friends or family, they gain a greater respect for this profession.

# The Bottom Line

Safety is a bedrock priority for many families, for obvious reasons. It affects the mindset of our children and families and has an impact on all the other priorities. Feeling unsafe affects a child's ability to focus and is a leading cause of separation anxiety and various stress-related disorders. Also, safety can affect student attendance. If parents do not feel the school is safe, they are not going to send their children to the school.

# Priority 4: Health

It is obvious that healthy children perform better in school, and so it is critical to ensure that all families have access to medical services that can help them deal with both chronic conditions, such as asthma and diabetes, and relatively minor illnesses, such as colds and flu. I grew up in a community with a high rate of asthma and diabetes, and I have family members who would miss days of school because of their health conditions. Even though they were successful, their many health-related challenges made it difficult for them to reach their potential. And I remember speaking to a specialist about how students with colds, stuffy noses, and ear infections may be unable to hear the sounds they need to know as part of early literacy development. The consequences could include poor performance in phonics and other developmental areas.

Families without access to medical insurance are often unable to provide the care needed to keep their children healthy. What if you could provide health services at the school? Imagine having a full-service clinic in the school with a dentist, doctor, ophthalmologist, psychologist, nurse, and social worker ready to meet all your children's health needs. Having such an on-site facility would increase your attendance, because students would not need to miss school for doctor or dentist appointments, and it would provide a much-needed service to your community, with benefits including peace of mind for parents and caregivers.

## Identifying the Gaps

When conducting the community-matching process with a focus on health, gathering data about your community is important so that you can identify the extent of health concerns such as asthma, diabetes, poor vision, hearing loss, sleep deprivation, and other conditions that are common in high-poverty communities. Privacy laws prevent access to information about individuals, but general information is available to the public. Building relationships with hospitals and health-care providers will give you access to data you need to be informed. You can also survey your community, reassuring respondents that all information provided will remain confidential.

Knowing the various health concerns that affect your community and matching those against available resources will reveal the gaps that you could fill through services provided within your school. Once you identify the gaps, you will be able to strategize which partners you need to bring into the school building.

Here are some questions to ask when identifying the gaps related to the health needs of your students and community:

- What are the primary diseases, illnesses, and other health conditions affecting your community?

- What resources, including hospitals and clinics, are available in your community to address these diseases, illnesses, and health concerns?

- Does the school have an on-site health clinic that addresses the gaps?

- Do you have an insurance provider that works in your community?

- Does the school have any medical professionals on staff, such as a nurse, who could treat minor health concerns?

## Specifying Needs

As described in the previous sections, health needs related to chronic diseases and illnesses must be a priority. However, there are also health-related government requirements that schools must meet. For example, many states require children to be immunized before they can attend school. Establishing a partnership with a health-care provider for schoolwide immunization could make it easy for families to meet this requirement, ensuring that schools are in full compliance. Other health needs, including those related to vision and hearing, have a direct impact on student learning. Your school may need to offer regular screenings to ensure that students are not suffering from hearing loss or a visual impairment. Early detection can have a major impact on student achievement.

Here are some questions to ask as you specify your health-related needs:

- How are health issues affecting student attendance, behavior, and performance?

- Do students receive regular screenings for hearing, vision, and dental health?

- Do you provide a way for families to get their children immunized, as required by state law?

- What difference might a school-based health clinic make for your students?

- Do you need a partnership with health and wellness organizations?

## Telling Your Story

When you visit organizations that you hope will support your efforts related to the health priority, it is important to have your story clearly defined, with your needs transparent. Here are two examples:

> The Bronx ranks 69th out of 69 counties in New York State when it comes to health conditions. Our borough is struggling to provide adequate health services to our families, and we must do something to change this situation for our children. If you establish a health clinic in our school, we will be able to better serve our community. We are willing to give you the space if you are willing to provide the service.
>
> More than 70 percent of our students suffer from asthma. As a result of this health condition, many of the students are on the chronic-absentee list. With your support, we hope to decrease the chronic absenteeism rate that negatively affects our students' performance.

Here are questions to help you craft your story:

- What are the demographics of your school community (race, ethnicity, socioeconomic status, etc.)?
- How can you quantify the lack of available health supports (e.g., number of health clinics in the community, distance to dental/medical clinics, access to health coverage)?
- How would you describe the quality of health care your families receive?
- How do health conditions or routine health care, such as doctor and dental appointments, affect attendance?
- How does your school community rank in the area of health compared with state or national averages?
- Do you need a clinic in your school? Why?
- What do you hope to accomplish through a health-related program or initiative?

## Establishing Strategic Partnerships

Once you have specified the health-related needs of the community and the most important areas of concern, you can determine which organizations you would like to partner with. For example, if a large percentage of students in your school suffer from asthma, you might want to establish a partnership with the asthma treatment program at a local hospital.

Nonprofit organizations are a promising avenue to pursue. For example, one of C.S. 55's main partners in the area of health and wellness is the Green Bronx Machine, which began as an after-school program for disconnected youth and, under the leadership of founder Stephen Ritz, has expanded into a broad-based organization that focuses on developing healthy communities through urban agriculture, including school and community gardens that provide healthy produce and employ local residents. In 2016, C.S. 55 and the Green Bronx Machine converted an empty space in the school into a National Health, Wellness, and Learning Center that exemplifies the belief that "healthy students are at the heart of healthy schools, and healthy schools are at the heart of healthy communities" (Green Bronx Machine, n.d.). The center includes an indoor teaching farm, an outdoor garden with irrigated raised beds, a media and resource center, and a classroom kitchen. It has been visited by representatives from around the world, highlighted in global media, and replicated at the U.S. Botanic Garden in Washington, D.C. More than 6,000 classrooms in the United States have since used the technology that was introduced at C.S. 55. Our students were even invited to the Obama White House, where they participated in planting indoor and outdoor gardens.

Sometimes the most productive partnerships are those you establish with individuals. For example, elected officials often have access to health-related funds, and they like to partner with schools around health and wellness issues. In addition, they may have staff members who have expertise in these areas.

Once you have identified possible partners, the next step is to arrange a meeting. I highly recommend that the principal, director, or head of school be the primary contact when first establishing the partnership. During the meeting, your goal is to discuss all the things you will need for the partnership to be successful. You will want to be sure that "your story" is focused on the services you would like the potential partner to provide. Also identify staff within your organization who may be interested in grant writing and can prepare applications to secure funds.

Here are questions to ask to help you find potential partners:

- Who are people you know personally who can help you address health and wellness issues?

- What community agencies and organizations, including nonprofits, address health issues?

- Are there hospitals, clinics, or other health providers that do community outreach?

- Who are the elected officials who have access to funds that can be used to improve the health conditions of the community?

# A Community-Matching Worksheet for the Health Priority

Completing the worksheet introduced in Chapter 1 can help you organize and record your community-matching efforts for the health priority. The worksheet has spaces for each part of the process: identifying the gaps between needs and available resources, specifying needs, telling your story, and establishing strategic partnerships. Figure 5.1 is an example of a completed worksheet for the health priority.

**FIGURE 5.1**

---

**Sample Community-Matching Worksheet for Priority 4: Health**

**Identifying the Gaps**
Through our community-matching process, we found that the school needs to provide health support for families. Many of our families suffer from chronic illnesses and poor health conditions. The community is lacking in health-care facilities, the air quality is poor, and the water needs constant treatment. It is hard to find high-quality, healthy food. Poor living conditions such as mold and rat infestations also lead to health issues such as asthma.

**Specifying Needs**
The community needs a health clinic to provide support to the families. If the school provides the space, a local hospital can create a school-based

health clinic for the community, with a nurse, dentist, psychologist, doctor, and ophthalmologist on staff. If we partner with a hospital, our students and families can get physical exams and immunizations on site, as well as rapid testing for COVID-19.

**Telling Your Story**
We serve the poorest congressional district in the United States. Many of our families live below the poverty level. The children do not have access to a health clinic in their community. If you put a school-based health clinic in our school, not only will you benefit financially, but our students will also receive a much-needed service. We have space for a health clinic in the building if you are willing to provide the service.

**Establishing Strategic Partnerships**
Possible partners to look into include elected officials, state and local health department staff, private donors, federal government agencies, health-care providers, hospitals, clinics, and other organizations that focus on health issues.

# Sample Projects

Here are descriptions of sample projects that address issues related to health and wellness. They may give you ideas for how your school can work on this priority.

## School-Based Health Clinics

If you have available space in your school building, you may be able to partner with hospitals that would be interested in using that space to create school-based health clinics. These clinics can serve as "mini-hospitals" in schools, providing an array of needed services.

## Schoolyards and Play Spaces

Work with elected officials, community leaders, and community-based organizations to design and fund a playground. The goal is to create a space where children can run, play, and engage in physical activities and sports. The community can also use the space for outdoor events and distribution of items such as food and clothing.

### Health and Wellness Centers

A partnership with an organization like the Green Bronx Machine can lead to the development of a health and wellness center like the one described in the section on establishing strategic partnerships.

### Community Gardens

You can convert outdoor spaces surrounding the school into community gardens using raised beds. You can use the gardens to teach children about the life cycle of plants as they go from planting seeds to harvesting vegetables. You can also invite families to participate in growing their own food.

### Health Fairs and Community Events

Health plans and insurance companies may be interested in sponsoring health fairs and other community events that can provide families with information and advice on health and wellness. For example, community leaders Gabriel DeJesus, Christina DeJesus, and Jay Pierre Ithier have worked collaboratively with health insurance company Healthfirst as long-standing partners of C.S. 55. More than 14 years ago, we started working together to address community health issues through our annual Community School 55 Back-to-School Event. Over the years, the event has grown to attract thousands of attendees. We give away 2,000 bookbags, lots of healthy food, and health kits. We also provide health screenings, physical activities, blood pressure checks, diabetes exams, and fire safety demonstrations. It's a fun event that helps support the health of the community.

## The Bottom Line

We know that poor health affects students' ability to focus on school and often leads to absenteeism. It can even affect children's ability to read, speak, and perform on grade level. Ensuring that children achieve to their highest potential requires us to recognize health as a top priority and take action to address the inequities in this area.

# Priority 5: Technology Access

The digital divide has been a problem since the earliest days of computer-based technology, and although the gap is narrowing, it continues to require our attention (Turner, 2016). According to a 2021 survey by the Pew Research Center (Atske & Perrin, 2021), 80 percent of white adults in the United States report having a traditional computer, compared with 69 percent of Black adults and 67 percent of Hispanic adults. Access to the internet reflects similar differences: 80 percent of whites report having home internet access, compared with 71 percent of Blacks and 65 percent of Hispanics. (In one encouraging sign, the survey found that the rate of ownership of smartphones and tablet computers was similar across the groups—about 85 percent for smartphones and about 53 percent for tablets.)

When it comes to the digital divide, we can learn from our past. In 1998, Betty A. Rosa was named superintendent of Community School District 8 in the Bronx. She inherited a district that was divided by race and economic status. The digital divide was evident in the communities she was serving. Ahead of her time, Rosa envisioned a district with no digital divide. She quickly reallocated resources to ensure that every family in her district would have access to technology and the internet. She formed a technology team under the leadership of Steven Rosenthal to launch an initiative called Homebase 8.

To accomplish her goal, Rosa partnered with local elected officials, including Rubén Díaz Jr. of the Bronx, who was then a state assemblyman and later became the Bronx borough president. Together, they worked to ensure that all the schools in his jurisdiction received adequate resources and computers. Every family with children attending school in District 8 received a brand-new iMac, provided a parent or other caregiver in the household had completed a four-day training.

Although the distribution of thousands of computers was a big step in the right direction, it revealed the need for adequate internet service. Some communities did not have internet access, and even if it was available, many families could not afford the high cost. The program secured internet access for the families by monetizing visits to the website and using the monies earned to purchase internet access from the local provider. Dr. Rosa, yet again a visionary, had her team start a website called Homebase 8 to provide the families with free or reduced-price access to the internet. Every time someone visited the Homebase 8 website, dollars were generated in an account that was used to purchase equipment and provide access for the families. The tech team also provided free tech support to families. Most of the funds for this initiative came from the New York City Council and other local sources.

In an important next step, the Homebase 8 tech team developed a remote curriculum that would be appealing to students. The curriculum covered all subject areas, including math, literacy, science, social studies, and the arts. The team created animated content that included games, instructional videos, and cartoons to engage the students. This was being done when this technology was new, and companies were just beginning to use it in this novel way. Yet again,

Dr. Rosa leveraged the internet to be able to self-sustain the program by generating funds from visits to the Homebase 8 website. The online content was available to all the students in District 8, and the website also provided resources for parents, including a weekly newsletter.

The work begun under Dr. Rosa, who is now the state commissioner of education and president of the University of the State of New York, continues today. Many of the issues that existed during her tenure as superintendent still exist in communities throughout the United States, and we must continue to fight against inequities related to technology access. Working together, we can end the digital divide so that all students have access to devices and all families have access to the internet.

## Identifying the Gaps

The community-matching process can begin by surveying your community to see who has access to technology, including access to the internet, and what kind of technology they use. At C.S. 55, before the launch of the Homebase 8 initiative, we found that many of our families did not have access to adequate technology.

Here are some questions to ask when identifying the technology gaps in your school and among the families you serve:

- What are the technology needs of your school community?
- What are the technology resources your school offers to the community?
- What technology resources does the surrounding community offer through libraries, community centers, and similar locations?
- What do you see when you compare needs and available resources?
- How does a lack of access to technology affect your students and community?
- What percentage of families qualify for free or reduced-price lunch? (This statistic can be an indicator of their ability to afford up-to-date technology devices and access to the internet.)

- What percentage of families do not have access at home to the kind of technology that is necessary for remote learning?

## Specifying Needs

Here are questions to ask as you determine what your school needs in the area of technology access:

- What percentage of children have access to up-to-date technology devices at home?
- What percentage of families have reliable internet access at home?
- Do all students have access to up-to-date technology in school?
- Do you need computer labs or upgrades to existing labs?
- Does the school have the electrical infrastructure to support a computer lab or upgraded lab?

## Telling Your Story

As with the other priorities, it is necessary to have a clear, persuasive story to share with potential partners who could support your efforts to close the technology gap. The story should include an explicit statement of what you are asking for and why. Here is an example:

> Many of our families do not have access to technology devices or the internet. It is important as a community to provide children with the needed technology to be successful in school. If you provide us with $85,000, we could upgrade the school's computer lab and purchase devices for the children who do not have them.

Here are some questions to ask as you prepare to write your story:

- What are the demographics of your school community (race, ethnicity, socioeconomic status, etc.)?
- How can you quantify the lack of available technology (insufficient number of devices, unreliable or nonexistent access to the internet)?
- How can you quantify the high price of technology, especially as it compares with the average household income in your community?

- How would you describe the quality of the technology that the school has now? Is the technology outdated? Is the internet access sufficient to support a large number of users at one time?
- What is it, specifically, that you are asking for?
- Why is technology important for students?
- Is technology access an issue in your larger community?
- How does not having access to technology affect student performance?
- How will technology access improve your school?

## Establishing Strategic Partnerships

Technology is an expensive investment—whether it's new technology or upgrades to existing resources. Therefore, it is critical to establish partnerships with potential funding sources.

Many local, state, and federal government agencies and programs are dedicated to technology initiatives, and they are a good starting point for identifying potential partners. Whenever possible, arrange for elected officials to visit your school so that they can see firsthand the need for investing in new or upgraded technology. Also inform them about families' specific needs for current technology devices and high-speed internet access.

Look for special federal funding initiatives, such as the i3 funding that was available during the Obama administration to achieve various goals, including improvements in low-achieving schools. Several technology-focused education organizations may provide grants, including the Bill & Melinda Gates Foundation and the George Lucas Educational Foundation. Other funding partners could be the philanthropic arms of businesses or organizations, such as the New York Yankees sports team mentioned in Chapter 4.

As with elected officials, it's advisable to have other potential partners visit your school to see the need for themselves. Coming face-to-face with the reality of outdated or limited technology is more powerful than a description in a letter or grant proposal.

That said, don't ignore the potential of social media to make your case. Most families and potential partners use social media for business and pleasure. Create accounts on Instagram, Facebook, LinkedIn, Twitter, and even TikTok. By using these platforms, you may find potential partners—and you will increase your parent engagement as well. Many of my grant and funding opportunities came through my social media presence. If you personally do not use social media platforms, you can turn to someone in your school who is proficient with them and willing to help. That person may also be able to assist with research to identify organizations that address issues related to technology access and any programs they might have for donating funds or devices.

Another option to consider as a funding source is DonorsChoose, a nonprofit organization that allows individuals to directly respond to teachers' requests for money for projects. You can organize a team of teachers or staff to write requests and post them on the DonorsChoose website (www.donorschoose.org).

Here are some questions to ask to help you identify potential partners:

- Does the organization have a history of donating funds for access to technology?

- Do the products the partner can provide meet the needs of the community? For example, does the technology support the programs used in the school?

- What is the partner willing to commit to? Is the contribution going to be a one-time donation or a long-term partnership?

- Where is the partner located? If it is local, does the partner have a history of philanthropy in the local community? If national, does it have a history of philanthropy in your geographical area or with your type of school (e.g., schools with your demographics or schools of your type, such as technology-focused magnet schools, and so on)?

- Do you know individuals who work in a technology-related field or in the philanthropy division of an organization? If so, create a list of their names and contact information.

# A Community-Matching Worksheet for the Technology Access Priority

Completing the worksheet introduced in Chapter 1 can help you organize and record your community-matching efforts for the technology priority. The worksheet has spaces for each part of the process: identifying the gaps between needs and available resources, specifying needs, telling your story, and establishing strategic partnerships. Figure 6.1 is an example of a completed worksheet for the technology priority.

## FIGURE 6.1

---

### Sample Community-Matching Worksheet for Priority 5: Technology Access

**Identifying the Gaps**

Through our community-matching process, we found that our families are in desperate need of improved access to technology, including internet access. During the COVID-19 pandemic, we realized that many of our families could not afford a device that their children could use to participate in remote learning through virtual classrooms. More than 60 percent of the children did not have an adequate device, and approximately 30 percent did not have internet access, including the families living in homeless shelters.

**Specifying Needs**

The community needs support to improve access to technology and, more specifically, the internet. Many of the families are sharing a phone or one other device to access the education resources provided by the school. Without devices and access to the internet, students are unable to complete classroom assignments and homework.

**Telling Your Story**

We serve the poorest congressional district in the United States. Many of our families live below the poverty level and depend on the school for their essentials. The children do not have the benefit of up-to-date technology, including devices and access to the internet. As a result, our children are at an academic disadvantage. In larger families, children must share the technology available at home, often using a single cell phone for academic and personal use. We must make sure all children have a device and internet access at home or in the shelter where they live.

*continued*

**FIGURE 6.1** *(continued)*

## Sample Community-Matching Worksheet
## for Priority 5: Technology Access

### Establishing Strategic Partnerships

We need to establish partnerships with elected officials and the state department of education to provide technology to all students. These partners have available funds to upgrade and supply new devices for the families. There is a process called Resolution A that can be used to request technology upgrades and devices. There are other possible partners like foundations, tech companies, and nonprofits that can also support our effort.

### *Elected officials*

New York State Assembly members, New York State senators, New York City borough presidents, New York City Council members

### *Foundations and nonprofits*

Bill & Melinda Gates Foundation, DonorsChoose.org, Rockefeller Foundation

### *Department of Education*

New York City Chancellor's Office, New York City Department of Education, New York City Office of Technology

### *Technology companies*

Adobe, Apple, Dell, Hewlett-Packard

## What We Learned from the Pandemic

The COVID-19 pandemic did not cause the inequities related to technology access; it just exposed them to a wider audience. There has always been a division between those who can afford the technology and those who cannot. This situation puts children who live in poverty at an obvious disadvantage, which was more evident during the pandemic, when schools were forced to close and instruction was offered only remotely. We saw that many schools—and teachers—were not prepared for this drastic change. Money that schools might have spent before the pandemic on improved technology and training that could be useful for remote learning was allocated to other important concerns—including, for example, mental health support provided by school counselors.

On the receiving end of remote learning, families experienced "broken instruction," or a period with inadequate instruction. Having to work virtually was particularly challenging for our children with special needs and English language learners. Many of these students found it difficult to sit at a computer for hours to receive instruction. Remote instruction also negatively affected our preK program. Most 3- and 4-year-olds lack the ability to sit at a computer and focus on the teacher. We also know that young students are dependent on schools to learn socialization skills, and the pandemic obviously made meeting that objective difficult, if not impossible. Simply stated, we learned that technology can never replace face-to-face interactions between teachers and students.

## Sample Projects

Here are descriptions of projects for increasing access to technology. Some of them address classroom needs and student experiences, and others demonstrate how technology can improve more general schoolwide efforts, including communication with families and others. They may give you ideas for how your school can address the technology priority.

### Equipment Upgrades for Media Labs and Laptop Carts

During the last few years, many schools have converted their libraries into media centers, incorporating computer labs and, in some cases, 3D printing labs. Other schools rely on carts that are loaded with laptops and can be easily moved from one classroom to another. In either case, the available equipment should be evaluated regularly to determine its usefulness and reliability.

## Interactive Whiteboards in Every Classroom

Interactive whiteboards are a useful tool for classroom instruction. They allow images to be projected from a computer to the board, and students can interact with the images using a special tool or even a finger. Many teachers find that the use of interactive whiteboards increases student engagement.

## Print Shops

Some schools have established their own print shops, equipped with large-scale printers that allow them to produce items they can use for marketing and branding, such as posters and banners. Some even create their own T-shirts and uniforms. Although the initial cost of the equipment may be high, schools save money over the long term and don't have to rely on outside shops.

## SchoolCNXT

SchoolCNXT (www.schoolcnxt.com) is a technology platform that makes it easy to connect with families. Among other things, it allows teachers to text parents and caregivers without having to share phone numbers. Also, the school can post announcements and talk directly to individuals. The platform provides an equitable means of communication with all families and helps to overcome barriers related to language and literacy.

## Educational Television

Establishing partnerships with local television stations can help you to provide instructional content and vital information to families. In the Bronx, a TV program called *The Bronx Edulution* is broadcast through a partnership with BronxNet, a public cable network that provides educational content and government access throughout the borough. In its season premiere in the fall of 2021, the show presented a segment for students about speaking and listening, a story-time event, and a piece about volcanoes. A statement on the BronxNet website explains the goal of *The Bronx Edulution*: "The program focuses on providing #Equity4All through high-quality creative learning opportunities, and seeks to ensure that no student is left behind during hybrid learning." Programs such as *The Bronx Edulution* also provide a great way for you to get visibility for your school and to share important information with your school families.

## The Bottom Line

Lack of equitable access to technology was made more evident during the pandemic, as many families struggled to work from home while their children faced the challenge of remote learning. However, the digital divide was a serious issue in many communities long before COVID-19. Although in some ways the situation has improved (ownership of smartphones, for example, is fairly equitable across racial groups), access to technology remains a critical concern for schools and families in high-poverty areas. Efforts by elected officials and others to address technology shortfalls have helped, but the need remains huge. Now, more than ever, we must sustain the gains we have made and close the gaps where they exist.

# Priority 6: Education

The Introduction to this book presents its key message: that it is important to understand that, for many families with children, education is not the first priority but the sixth priority, after food, shelter, safety, health, and access to technology. All these priorities are intertwined, and as we try to educate the whole child, we see that they overlap in many ways and have a direct impact on whether we achieve our goals. To succeed, we must spend time and energy addressing the inequities that exist in these priorities.

The sixth priority, education, is a complex matter, with many areas of focus that compete for attention and funding. Deciding which areas to concentrate on will depend on your school and community. However, this chapter will discuss four areas that are often underfunded and that we must focus on to truly educate the whole child and end many of the inequities that we have talked about in the previous chapters. These areas are mental health, literacy, culturally relevant education, and sports and arts programs. Many schools in high-poverty communities struggle to fund these areas (as well as other education initiatives) because dollars must be allocated to other priorities. This struggle perpetuates the inequities between students in these communities and their counterparts in places with higher socioeconomic status. These inequities put children at a disadvantage and ultimately hurt them.

## MENTAL HEALTH

Addressing the social-emotional needs of our community is essential. Living in a high-poverty, high-crime community brings many challenges for our families, and many, if not all, of the children in those families suffer from some form of mental health concern. As educators, we must acknowledge the anxieties that children bring to school daily and find ways to help them. We cannot expect to succeed in educating our children without addressing their mental health needs.

## Identifying the Gaps

When conducting the community-matching process with a focus on mental health, it is important to learn about your community by gathering data. Poverty rates will likely correlate with the rate of mental health issues. Families who face hunger, poverty, and, in many cases, homelessness are more likely to experience various health issues, including those related to mental health. Another major factor affecting mental health is the community's crime rate. Many of our children are exposed to violence and other illegal activities that have a major impact on how they view the world.

Here are some questions to ask when evaluating the mental health needs of your students and community:

- What are the statistics related to mental health needs of your school community?
- What are the resources your school offers to the community?
- What resources does the community have to offer?

- Does your school have a mental health clinic on the premises?
- Are there health plans available in your community that provide mental health support?
- Does your school have social workers and counselors available for students and their families?
- Does your school have a psychologist?
- Are there clinics or a hospital in the immediate community?

## Specifying Needs

Many issues compete for our attention, but mental health is a priority we need to address so that our children can focus on their academic learning. Doing so can require making difficult choices. For example, at C.S. 55, we wanted to upgrade our computer lab, but we decided to delay that initiative until we made sure our mental health supports were in place.

Here are questions to consider as you specify your needs related to the mental health of your students:

- Does your community have mental health clinics?
- Do you need a school-based mental health clinic?
- Do you need to establish a partnership with a mental health organization?
- What mental health issues do you need to address?
- Are there community-based organizations with mental health programs available in the surrounding area?
- Do you have funds to pay for mental health services for your students and their families?

## Telling Your Story

As with all priorities, it is important to have a clear, credible story that outlines your situation and needs. Potential partners will want to know why they should work with your school and what you expect to achieve through the partnership. Here is an example of a story:

We serve the poorest congressional district in the United States, with one of the highest crime rates in New York City. More than 98 percent of our children live below the poverty line, and our school is located in a high-crime area. Due to these demographics, many of our families are faced with mental health issues. Unfortunately, our students and their families do not have access to a mental health clinic in the neighborhood. If you put a mental health clinic in our school, you will be able to increase the number of clients you serve, and our students will receive a much-needed service.

Here are questions to help you write your story:

- What are the demographics of your school community (race, ethnicity, socioeconomic status, etc.)?

- How can you quantify the lack of available mental health clinics or community-based organizations that include mental health services?

- How would you describe the quality of mental health services provided to your families?

- Why is mental health an issue in your community?

- How does poor mental health affect attendance, behavior, and achievement?

- Where does your school community rank in the area of mental health compared with other communities?

- Do you need to provide mental health support services within your school? Why?

- What do you hope to accomplish in your effort to improve the mental health of your students and their families?

- What are the negative impacts on students who are struggling with mental health issues?

## Establishing Strategic Partnerships

Elected officials at the federal, state, and local levels have made it known that mental health is a priority that must be addressed, and it is likely that funding for this purpose will increase in the coming years. It is important for educators to identify and assign an individual or a team of people to lobby for access to these funds and to complete applications for grants that become available. You can do the same with various nonprofit organizations dedicated to mental health issues.

Once you have identified the partners you want to work with and have written your story, arrange an in-person meeting with one or more representatives of the organization. As with other priorities, I highly recommend that the principal, director, or head of school be the primary contact when first establishing the partnership. At the meeting, discuss all the things you will need for the partnership to be successful.

Here are questions to help you identify potential partners:

- Are there people you already know who might be able to help you address mental health issues?

- Which organizations and agencies in your community address mental health?

- Are there hospitals and clinics in the community that you could approach about a partnership?

- Who are the elected officials who have control over funds that can be used to improve the mental health conditions of the community?

## A Community-Matching Worksheet for the Mental Health Priority

Completing the worksheet introduced in Chapter 1 can help you organize and record your community-matching efforts for the mental health priority. The worksheet has spaces for each part of the process: identifying the gaps between needs and available resources, specifying needs, telling your story, and finding possible partners. Figure 7.1 is an example of a completed worksheet for the mental health priority.

## FIGURE 7.1

---

## Sample Community-Matching Worksheet
## for Priority 6: Education/Mental Health

### Identifying the Gaps

Through our community-matching process, we found that the school needs to provide mental health support for families. Many of our families live below the poverty line, and the school is located in a high-crime area. The families are constantly exposed to traumatic events, and the COVID-19 pandemic made the situation worse. Our school and community currently do not have sufficient mental health supports in place.

### Specifying Needs

The community needs support in providing children and their families with access to mental health supports. The school needs to establish a partnership with a community-based organization or create a mental health clinic in the building. We need to increase the number of school counselors who are qualified to address students' mental health needs or can refer them to other sources of care.

### Telling Your Story

We serve the poorest congressional district in the United States. Many of our families live below the poverty level. Our school is also located in a high-crime area. These circumstances have contributed to the ongoing trauma that many of our children experience. Our students and their families do not have access to a mental health clinic in the neighborhood. If you put a mental health clinic in our school, you will be able to increase the number of clients you serve, and our students will receive a much-needed service. We have space available in the building for such a clinic if you are willing to provide the service.

### Establishing Strategic Partnerships

Possible partners to look into include elected officials, state and local health department staff, private donors, federal government agencies, mental health providers, hospitals, clinics, and other organizations that focus on mental health issues.

### What We Learned from the Pandemic

The pandemic did not create the mental health issues that exist in our communities, but it did compound them and make them more visible. Many children were experiencing trauma before COVID-19, but the disease caused additional health-related concerns that elevated their trauma to a higher level. The number of people becoming ill and dying from the virus put our children and community in a state of fear. An invisible enemy overwhelmed them, especially as children were no longer allowed to go outside and families felt trapped in their homes with no opportunities to breathe fresh air and release energy.

The pandemic alerted us to the importance of grief counseling as a way to help our families deal with the many deaths they experienced. Sadly, we must often deal with this issue when someone is killed as a result of criminal activity. The pandemic, however, made death a more frequent occurrence, and many of our families were not provided support for dealing with this crisis. We need to address that failure.

# Sample Projects

Initiatives to address mental health issues come in many forms. Here are descriptions of projects in this area. They may give you ideas for how your school can work on this priority.

## School-Based Mental Health Clinics

If you have available space in your building, you can invite hospitals to use that space to create school-based mental health clinics. These could be available to students and their families by appointment on certain days and at certain hours, depending on the hospital's available resources. The more you invest in this initiative, the more resources hospitals can provide.

## Safe Spaces

You can create spaces in the school where children can go to get away from stressful situations in the classroom or elsewhere—for example, after an angry confrontation with another student. Such spaces should have couches, technology, toys, and other fun, age-appropriate items that make it comfortable and welcoming and that help students relax. You could even include a punching bag to help students release negative energy. You can make these spaces available for parents as well as students.

## Health and Wellness Center

Nonprofit organizations can provide support for health and wellness centers that encourage children and families to take part in exercise and provide information on healthy eating. In the Bronx, a nonprofit called the Green Bronx Machine has supported this kind of effort, as described in Chapter 5. (For more information, visit www.greenbronxmachine.org.)

## Community Gardens and Farms

If you have space in the grounds outside your school or on the rooftop, you can convert it into a community garden that will not only provide food for students and their families but also create a pleasant, soothing place for students to spend time. School gardens have the additional benefit of providing a hands-on way for students to learn about the life cycle of plants. You may be able to partner with organizations focused on diabetes or other diet-related conditions to get the funding to create and maintain a community garden.

## Health Fairs

Health insurance companies can be asked to sponsor health fairs or be present at other community events, where they can provide information on various aspects of physical and mental well-being. Schools do not need to use their own funds to provide these activities.

The sponsoring organizations will benefit from the exposure they gain in the community.

## LITERACY

Literacy is foundational to all learning, so it is paramount that we consider ways to address student achievement gaps in this area. Literacy is a concern for all students, but lack of literacy disproportionately affects Black and Hispanic students.

Lack of literacy is a key indicator for students dropping out, and dropout rates are strongly correlated to incarceration rates. This fact captures the essence of the school-to-prison pipeline issue mentioned in the Introduction to this book. Consider the following observations from an article in *The Atlantic*:

> In an *Education Week* article last year, the magazine highlighted a report by sociology professor Donald Hernandez who compared reading scores and graduation rates of almost 4,000 students. "A student who can't read on grade level by 3rd grade is four times less likely to graduate by age 19 than a child who does read proficiently by that time. Add poverty to the mix, and a student is 13 times less likely to graduate on time than his or her proficient, wealthier peer," read the report. Couple that with a study comparing dropout rates and incarceration rates in *The New York Times*, and one could draw a strong connection. The study by researchers at Northeastern University used a range of census data to find that "about one in every 10 young male high school dropouts is in jail or juvenile detention, compared with one in 35 young male high school graduates." (Hudson, 2012, paras. 6–7)

As we work to end the inequities of the world, we must continue to try to dismantle the school-to-prison pipeline. Too many of our Black and Brown youth find that school is more likely to be a path to prison than to college and careers.

We must work to redirect this path, and it all starts with early interventions to ensure that students are proficient in reading. In particular, we must emphasize phonemic awareness and make phonics a priority in all schools. We know that families who have access to many resources start teaching their children how to read at an early age. When I first became the principal of C.S. 55, I was told that the preK program was only for socialization, and math and English language arts should not be part of the curriculum. Although many people will argue that socialization should be the focus in early childhood education, I strongly believe that we cannot afford to wait to educate our children in the basic elements of literacy.

## Identifying the Gaps

When conducting the community-matching process for literacy initiatives, gathering data is an important first step. Collect information on your students' literacy skills and compare it with national averages or with statistics from other schools in your state or in nearby communities. We know that many of our youth do not perform on a level with their peers in the area of literacy, and assembling the facts about the deficiencies is a good starting point for making sure that all children have access to equitable resources and instruction.

Here are some questions to ask when evaluating the literacy needs of your students and community:

- What do statistics, such as test scores, reveal about the needs of your school community in the area of literacy?
- What percentage of your students are performing at grade level?
- What are the literacy resources, including staff and materials, your school offers to students?
- What resources does the surrounding community have to offer?
- Is your school's attendance rate affecting student performance?
- Do you have after-school programs in your community that could support literacy (for example, story time at a local library)?
- Are your classroom libraries adequate?
- Does your school have funds to buy books for classroom libraries?
- Are your teachers trained in literacy instruction?

## Specifying Needs

Many of our schools are struggling more than ever to provide high-quality literacy programs. In the wake of the pandemic, schools are reopening with fewer teachers and support staff and inadequate resources. At times like this, anything on our wish list that is intended to beautify our schools should be set aside for more important concerns. Given the fundamental importance of literacy for success in every other aspect of life, we must focus on ensuring our students are acquiring the necessary skills in this area.

Here are some questions to consider when specifying needs related to literacy:

- Do you need a school library?
- Do you need a partnership with a community-based organization to get funding and other resources for your efforts to improve literacy?
- Do you need classroom libraries?
- What, specifically, do you need to support your students' literacy development?
- Do you need technology—devices and apps—to support your students and teachers in learning and teaching literacy?

## Telling Your Story

When you visit the organizations that you hope will support your efforts related to literacy, it is important to have your story ready to share, with relevant background information and clearly defined needs. Here is an example:

> We serve a community that has a high crime rate. The incarceration rate affecting our families is one of the highest in New York City. We view education—and literacy programs, in particular—as a means of providing opportunities for our students so that they can pursue college and careers and avoid being part of the cycle of failure and the school-to-prison pipeline that has plagued our community. As part of our literacy efforts, we are seeking funds to purchase books and other materials

for our school and classroom libraries, to staff an after-school reading program, and to train teachers and aides on academic interventions that will address the literacy needs of our students.

Here are questions to ask to help you write your story:

- What are the demographics of your school community (race, ethnicity, socioeconomic status, etc.)?
- How would you describe the quality of literacy programs in your school? Do you have statistics related to their effectiveness?
- Why is literacy an issue in your community?
- How does attendance affect your literacy rates?
- How does your school rank in the area of literacy compared with other schools in the community, the state, and the nation?
- Do you need to establish a library in your school or expand or improve an existing library?
- What specific resources do you need to accomplish your literacy goals?
- What, specifically, do you hope to accomplish in the area of literacy?
- What percentage of your students struggle with literacy? What are the consequences of their lack of literacy skills?

## Establishing Strategic Partnerships

Many elected officials understand that their constituents value literacy, and they are willing to partner with schools to develop or improve early-literacy programs and add to available resources, including technology such as computer-based reading programs and phone apps. Community-based organizations are also potential partners, including public libraries.

Here are questions to help you identify potential partners:

- Who are people in the community who might be able to help you get resources to improve literacy in your school?
- What are some local, state, and national organizations that address literacy issues?

- What community-based organizations are devoted to literacy or have literacy-related programs within their larger cluster of services?

- Are there elected officials who have control over funds that can be used to improve the literacy of the community?

- Have any of your elected officials supported literacy programs in the past?

- Does your curriculum require library materials, technology, or other resources that a local business could supply?

## A Community-Matching Worksheet for the Literacy Priority

Completing the worksheet introduced in Chapter 1 can help you organize and record your community-matching efforts for the literacy priority. The worksheet has spaces for each part of the process: identifying the gaps between needs and available resources, specifying needs, telling your story, and finding possible partners. Figure 7.2 is an example of a completed worksheet for the literacy priority.

**FIGURE 7.2**

---

**Sample Community-Matching Worksheet for Priority 6: Education/Literacy**

**Identifying the Gaps**
Through our community-matching process, we found that our school needs support in the area of literacy. We do not have a school library, and our classroom libraries need more books. We also need new computers or laptops so that our students and teachers can access online resources related to literacy.

**Specifying Needs**
Our school needs funds for a school library and expanded classroom libraries. We need to upgrade our technology so that our students and teachers have computers or laptops to access websites that provide digital resources for literacy instruction.

**Telling Your Story**

We serve the poorest congressional district in the United States. Many of our families live below the poverty level. The children do not have access to literacy resources, books, or up-to-date technology that would enable them to access digital tools related to literacy. Our community also has a high crime rate that corresponds directly with a high incarceration rate. We believe there is a direct link between literacy and behavior that leads to criminal activity. We see an improved literacy program as one way to help dismantle the school-to-prison pipeline that has had such a negative impact on our families.

**Establishing Strategic Partnerships**

Possible partners to look into include elected officials, community-based organizations, after-school programs, community centers, churches, and public libraries.

## What We Learned from the Pandemic

The pandemic exposed what many educators already knew: that many children lack basic literacy skills, including the ability to read, and the shortcomings are particularly alarming among Black and Hispanic students. According to *Education Week,*

> The data on the foundational literacy skills of the class of 2032—the children who were in kindergarten during the shutdown and 1st graders during this bumpy and inequitable 2020–21 school year—are terrifying. According to one commonly used reading assessment, the DIBELS benchmark measures, the percentage of students falling into the "well-below benchmark" category that predicts future reading failure grew from 26 percent in December 2019 to 43 percent in December 2020. All demographic subgroups were affected, but Black and Hispanic students were particularly impacted. There is no precedent for this kind of decline in the last 20 years of using these reading measures. (Freitag, 2021, para. 3)

# Sample Projects

Literacy initiatives can take many forms. Here are descriptions of some sample projects for addressing literacy issues. They may give you ideas for how you can work on this priority at your school.

## Interactive Whiteboards

Many students learn best with the use of technology. Every classroom should have an interactive whiteboard for teachers to use to improve students' educational experience—including literacy activities. As described in Chapter 6, interactive whiteboards allow an image to be projected from a teacher's computer to the board, so that all students can see it. For literacy, for example, the image might show a sample text with errors for the students to identify. The teacher can use a tool to manipulate the text and model for the students how to make corrections. The teacher can also use the whiteboard to show instructional videos or conduct quick assessments.

## Audio Enhancement

Developing students' listening skills is often overlooked in favor of reading and writing. That's a mistake. Constructing meaning from sound is a crucial aspect of strong literacy skills. Audio enhancement devices, such as wearable microphones, help to amplify a teacher's voice so that students can clearly hear what the teacher is saying. This enhancement can be critical to ensuring that students acquire the fundamental elements of literacy—for example, the correct pronunciation of words. It also makes it easier for students to hear instructions for completing in-class or homework assignments. Systems are available that work even when teachers are wearing masks.

## Instructional Coaches

Instructional coaches who specialize in literacy can provide valuable support to classroom teachers. Some school districts provide such coaches at no additional expense to the school; in other cases, schools need to secure funding to establish and fill these positions.

## Digital Books

At C.S. 55, we use a program called myON that provides personal libraries of digitized books that are matched to individual students' reading level, interests, and grade level. This program allows children to access thousands of books through their laptops, computers, or phones. An audio option enables them to hear the words while they follow the written text. The easy access is especially beneficial to students who might find it difficult to go to the local public library because of distance or other barriers. All students, including English language learners, benefit. (Visit www.renaissance.com/products/myon for more information.)

## Caferary

At C.S. 55, we created a "caferary"—a cafeteria with books available for students to borrow. This project has allowed us to maximize our use of space and provide children with access to books during their lunch periods.

## Create a Library

If your school doesn't have a separate library, creating one is a worthwhile effort. It is important to create spaces where children can interact with books and develop a love for reading. At C.S. 55, we have a brand-new library that was funded by a grant we received from The Home Depot; the ribbon cutting happened in September 2022. We are continuing to write grants to make this place even more special.

# CULTURALLY RELEVANT EDUCATION

When educating youth, it is important to incorporate cultural elements of the surrounding community, particularly in the arts and in social studies classes. Educational resources and instruction should acknowledge the culture of the community you serve. At C.S. 55, the main cultural theme is hip hop. We are located in the Bronx, widely embraced as the birthplace of hip hop, and many of our families as well as those in other urban communities can relate to the cultural elements of hip hop. Other schools might focus on the cultures of ethnic groups within the school population, including African, Asian, Caribbean, Latin American, Middle Eastern, and other identities, celebrating their traditions, food, arts, and language. We must teach children about their own culture before we begin to teach them about others. I am not saying we should not teach children about the other cultures of the world; I am saying we should make it a priority to teach the children about their own culture.

## Identifying the Gaps

Identifying the gaps related to culturally relevant education requires that you first have an accurate picture of the cultural makeup of the school community. You can then look at things such as curriculum and classroom materials to see whether they acknowledge the school's cultural diversity. In addition, you can consider things such as hallway displays, the food served in the cafeteria, the arts programs, and the staff makeup. The point to remember is that creating an environment that respects the culture of the school community is not only about the books you use. Yes, you want books that reflect the community and the languages the families speak, but culturally relevant education is about more than just materials. It requires looking at the whole school and identifying the gaps in its recognition of the school's cultural makeup.

Here are some questions to ask when identifying the gaps in your school's effort to reflect the culture of your students and community:

- What countries do your families come from?
- What languages do your families speak?
- What foods do your students eat at home?
- Is there a dominant religion?
- Are there community leaders from the various cultural groups who can collaborate with the school to create culturally relevant education?
- Does the school have staff who speak the various languages your families speak?
- Do classroom materials reflect the community you serve?
- Does the schedule or calendar match the needs and honor the cultures of the community?

## Specifying Needs

To serve your community effectively, you must identify those things that you truly need in order to offer students a culturally relevant education. If your school resources do not meet the cultural needs of the community, you must adjust the curriculum, the physical environment (such as classroom and hall displays), the food served, the programming, the hiring practices, and much more.

Here are questions to help you identify needs in the area of culturally relevant education:

- Do you need translation services?
- Does the cafeteria menu need to be adjusted?
- Are there staff members who speak the languages of the community?
- Do you have staff who represent the community you serve?
- Do you need to adjust the schedule or calendar to accommodate the community?
- Is it necessary for you to purchase new books that better reflect students' cultures?
- Do you need to partner with a religious institution?
- Is there a space at the school that could be accessible to the community for cultural events?

## Telling Your Story

When you are looking for partners to help achieve your goals for culturally relevant education, it is important to have your story clearly defined, with your needs transparent. Here is an example:

> We serve the poorest congressional district in the United States, with an influx of immigrants coming from African countries. Many of these families do not speak English, and they come with unique needs. We need to purchase materials in their various languages, adjust our curriculum to acknowledge their culture, and provide them with social service programs. We will need funds to purchase new materials, provide an after-school program, and create an office to provide the families with social service support.

Here are questions to ask to help you write your story:

- What are the demographics of your school community (race, ethnicity, socioeconomic status, etc.)?
- What countries do your families come from?
- What are the cultures that make up your community?
- How does culture affect attendance?
- What music and arts do the families engage in?
- Do you have a space to support the families by providing social services?
- What do you hope to accomplish in the area of culturally relevant education?
- Does religion play an important role in the lives of the families you serve? Does it impact them negatively?
- What adjustments do you need to make to improve families' school experience?
- Why is focusing on culture important?
- What do you need to truly support your community in the area of culturally relevant education?

## Establishing Strategic Partnerships

Elected officials often like to partner with schools to help them meet the cultural needs of the community. They enjoy celebrating and recognizing the cultures of the people they serve. They can become partners in providing funds for various community activities, programs, and events. When considering potential partners, it is also important to know what role religion plays in the lives of families. At C.S. 55, for example, the school community includes a large Muslim population, which led us to partner with the local mosque. You can also partner with nonprofits and community-based programs that may provide resources that match the cultural needs of your families.

Here are questions to help you identify potential partners:

- Who are people you already know who might be able to help?
- What local or regional organizations work with the cultures you serve?

- Are there community-based organizations or nonprofits specifically aligned with the cultural groups you serve?
- Are there elected officials who could be partners, including anyone whose cultural background matches a culture represented by your families?
- Are there religious institutions in your community that could provide support?
- Does your community have restaurants that serve foods associated with your school's cultures and might be interested in donating food or participating in school events?
- Who are potential partners who could support after-school programs?
- What government officials and agencies could help support your efforts to offer culturally relevant education?

## A Community-Matching Worksheet for the Culturally Relevant Education Priority

Completing the worksheet introduced in Chapter 1 can help you organize and record your community-matching efforts to provide culturally relevant education. The worksheet has spaces for each part of the process: identifying the gaps between needs and available resources, specifying needs, telling your story, and finding possible partners. Figure 7.3 is an example of a completed worksheet for this priority.

**FIGURE 7.3**

---

**Sample Community-Matching Worksheet for Priority 6: Education/Culturally Relevant Education**

**Identifying the Gaps**

Through our community-matching process, we found that our school must provide an environment that is culturally relevant and meets the needs of our families. Many of our families come from Africa, specifically The Gambia, and they are struggling to assimilate to our school community. Currently our staff and resources do not match their needs.

*continued*

**FIGURE 7.3** (continued)

## Sample Community-Matching Worksheet for Priority 6: Education/Culturally Relevant Education

### Specifying Your Needs

As a community school with a large African community, we need to make adjustments to our programming, curriculum, food service, materials, and hiring practices. We need more staff in the building who speak the various languages represented among our students and who reflect the diverse school community we serve. We also need to create a space in the school where the families can be provided with information and access to resources in their home languages.

### Telling Your Story

We serve the poorest congressional district in the United States. Many of our families live below the poverty level. Every year, we enroll students from families arriving in our community from various countries, primarily The Gambia. These families have unique cultural and religious needs that we cannot address with our current resources. We need funds to provide the children with equitable opportunities to be successful. We need to purchase books and other resources and create a space where families can come for support from people who are familiar with their culture.

### Establishing Strategic Partnerships

Possible partners to look into include elected officials, government organizations, private donors, nonprofits, community-based organizations, embassies, restaurants, and religious institutions.

## What We Learned from the Pandemic

Our African community struggled during the COVID-19 pandemic. Many of our families come from The Gambia and Ghana. English is not their first language, so communicating with the families was difficult, and we had to hire staff members to provide translation support. In addition, out of safety concerns, some families did not want their children to attend school even after we reopened, which negatively affected attendance. Also, the families depend on the fathers working to provide food, but work became scarce during the pandemic, so access to food became a major issue. C.S. 55 partnered with a local food pantry to provide food for these families, but unfortunately, many of the services the African community depended on us to provide were unavailable during the pandemic. The confluence of these factors meant many families had no choice but to move back to Africa.

# Sample Projects

Creating a culturally relevant environment at your school can involve a variety of projects and initiatives. Here are descriptions of projects that illustrate how you can address the cultural needs of your community. They may give you ideas for addressing this priority at your school.

## Welcome Center

At C.S. 55, we partnered with an organization called Cultural African Preservation to meet the needs of our African community. The organization created an office in the school that is staffed by volunteers, community leaders, and school staff who speak the various languages represented in the school. Our hope is that this welcome center will increase school attendance of African and African American students, create a respectful environment, and encourage their families to be involved in the school.

## Culturally Sensitive Menus

Food is connected directly to the various cultures we serve, and it is important to know the dietary needs and restrictions of the community. For example, in communities with large Muslim populations like ours, the school menu does not include pork products but, instead, offers plant-based proteins, chicken, or beef. Understanding and respecting the dietary needs of your school community is a crucial aspect of culturally relevant and sensitive education.

## Music and Arts Programs

The music and arts of the community must be supported and reflected in the school. (See the next section for more on this topic.)

The school's location and cultural makeup will determine what music and arts programs you should offer. In the case of C.S. 55, it made sense to focus on hip hop because the Bronx, where the school is located, is the birthplace of hip hop. In schools serving a large number of students from a certain ethnic group—Bengalis, for example—the music and art forms of that group should be incorporated into instruction. I am not saying schools should focus exclusively on music and other arts that reflect the community, but it is important that children come to know their own culture before they learn about others.

## Connections with Religious Institutions

Many families look to their churches, synagogues, and mosques for support. These institutions are often willing to partner with schools to build connections and understanding. We have created mentorship programs and other opportunities in partnership with religious institutions to better serve our community. For example, when we noticed that boys from our African community were demonstrating a lack of respect toward our female teachers, we had the idea of asking the imam from a mosque in the community to come to the school weekly to provide us with support. Soon, every month, a group of men from the African community would come in to talk to the youth about the importance of respecting their teachers. The mentorship program also gave us ideas on how to work better with our students. We learned important dates in the Islamic calendar, fasting days, and prayer times. Many of the issues had arisen out of a mutual lack of cultural understanding.

## Celebrations

At C.S. 55, we celebrate the various cultures that exist in our community. We hold cultural festivals, we celebrate the various languages spoken by members of our school community, and we have special events to provide families with resources. Every year, through our partnership with the Cultural African Preservation organization, we provide students with laptops for middle and high school. We also hold food and clothing drives specifically for our African community. It is important to find opportunities to acknowledge the music, art, food, religion, and languages of the people you serve.

## SPORTS AND ARTS PROGRAMS

Sports and arts programs have great power in our communities. Engaging children in physical activities and the arts contributes to a healthy lifestyle and opens up many opportunities for them to be successful in nonacademic aspects of life. Sports and arts education is not just about exposing children to these fields but also about inspiring and nurturing those who are interested in pursuing careers in these areas. Cutting sports and arts programs from school budgets should never be allowed; instead, they should be a priority.

Sadly, sports and arts programs are yet another example of the inequities in society. In affluent communities, parents can afford to pay for private lessons and to support sports leagues and other opportunities for their children. High-income communities tend to have sports centers, community centers that include sports and arts programs, soccer fields, baseball programs, tennis courts, golf courses, swimming pools, hockey rinks, and many other places where children can focus their energy in a positive way. The absence of such facilities in many urban neighborhoods—and the resulting lack of positive opportunities for youth engagement—is one reason these communities have such a high crime rate. Too many communities are underinvested when it comes to serving their young people. When we talk about education in communities of poverty, we must make sports and arts a priority.

There are many examples of how sports and arts have positively affected the lives of our Black and Brown youth. Whenever sports figures or artists talk about overcoming adversity, they discuss how a sport or an art form gave them an outlet and saved their lives. It is amazing to hear the stories of young men and women who grew up in a single-parent household or otherwise challenging situation yet were able to succeed because they were focused on an art or a sport. The benefits of involvement in such activities is huge—including for children's mental health.

Someone once asked me what could be done to increase the number of Black baseball players in the major leagues. I thought about it for a moment and took the person to what had once been a baseball field but was now being used as a dog park. I had never seen anyone playing sports on the baseball field. The field had not been maintained, and no one had invested in a baseball program in the community. I turned to the individual and said, "If you want more Black baseball players, invest in the Black communities, build those baseball fields, and develop programs."

## Identifying the Gaps

As with the other priorities, knowing your community is important for identifying the gaps in available resources and services dedicated to sports and arts programs. Too often, communities have no programs, or the ones they have lack skilled personnel, including qualified teachers and coaches. In addition to shortcomings in school programs, such as having no gyms, sports fields, or spaces for creating and presenting art, these communities may also lack high-quality community centers and arts institutions that could supplement what the school provides. Sports and arts programs can be costly, and even if they are available, many families struggle to pay for their children to participate.

Here are some questions to ask when evaluating the sports and arts needs of your students and community:

- Is there a community center in your surrounding neighborhood?
- Does your school have a gym?
- Do you have any after-school programs dedicated to sports and arts?
- Are health and physical fitness issues in your community?

- Given the choice, how would you know which arts and sports programs to prioritize?

- Do you have a community park near the school that could be used for sports or arts programs?

## Specifying Needs

Access to sports and arts programs is not just about the recreational value they provide but also about their potential to lead to scholarship opportunities that could determine whether a student will go to college. Knowledge and skills gained through arts program can also affect admission to specialized schools. Far from being just a *want*, sports and arts programs can be part of what students *need* in order to move forward with their education and lives as adults.

- Do you have the resources you need for sports and arts programs?

- Do you have staff who are qualified to teach music, visual arts, and other elements of an arts program?

- Do you have sports coaches?

- Could volunteers supplement the staff you have available for sports and arts?

- Do you need to partner with an arts institution?

- Does the community have sports and arts programs that could supplement what the school offers?

## Telling Your Story

When you visit organizations and individuals that could be potential partners, it is important to have a clearly defined story to share, with your needs specified. Here is an example:

> Our school does not have a gym or other sports facility or a quality arts program. The larger community also lacks a facility that could provide such programs. Without the school providing sports and arts programs, our children will not be able to participate in these developmentally

important activities. The lack of programs will limit their access to other opportunities and, sadly, without options for positive activities, many of our youth will turn to negative behaviors. We serve a community with a high crime rate, which we believe is due in part to the lack of programs to engage our youth.

Here are questions to help you write your story:

- What are the demographics of your school community (race, ethnicity, socioeconomic status, etc.)?

- How can you quantify the lack of available programs in the community?

- How would you describe the quality of the sports and arts programs currently provided by your school and by the larger community?

- Why is a lack of sports and arts programs an issue in your community?

- Are there links between students' health and the absence of sports programs at your school?

- Do you need a gym in your school? Why?

- What do you hope to accomplish through sports and arts programs?

- What benefits do you expect for your students as a result of providing these programs?

## Establishing Strategic Partnerships

Sports and arts programs can be highly visible in the community, and that makes them appealing to elected officials eager to show their support. Professional sports organizations and local businesses are other potential partners, along with community-based organizations dedicated to the arts. Police and fire departments may also be interested in getting involved—for example, by providing sports uniforms. Sports and arts organizations may be able to provide not only direct funding but also information about grants and other opportunities to support your efforts.

Here are questions to help you identify potential partners:

- Who are people you know who could provide support?

- Does your community have any professional sports teams?

- Are there businesses in your community that could cover the costs of sports equipment and uniforms or musical instruments?

- Are there local arts institutions that could provide help with developing arts programs?

- Does your community have public places where student art could be displayed? If so, who is in charge of those places?

- Who are the elected officials or agency staff members who distribute funds for the arts?

- Who are the elected officials or agency staff members who control funding that could be used to create sports centers, playfields, and gyms?

## A Community-Matching Worksheet for the Sports and Arts Programs Priority

Completing the worksheet introduced in Chapter 1 can help you organize and record your community-matching efforts for the sports and arts programs priority. The worksheet has spaces for each part of the process: identifying the gaps between needs and available resources, specifying needs, telling your story, and finding possible partners. Figure 7.4 is an example of a completed worksheet for this priority.

**FIGURE 7.4**

---

**Sample Community-Matching Worksheet for Priority 6: Education/Sports and Arts Programs**

**Identifying the Gaps**

Through our community-matching process, we found that our school needs to provide sports and arts opportunities for our families. Many of our families live below the poverty line and cannot afford to pay for private programs. The school currently does not have sports and arts programs, although the surrounding community does have some.

*continued*

**FIGURE 7.4** *(continued)*

## Sample Community-Matching Worksheet for Priority 6: Education/Sports and Arts Programs

### Specifying Needs
The school needs to provide sports and arts programs for a variety of reasons, including giving students equitable access to opportunities for college scholarships and admission to specialized schools, such as arts academies. These programs also have a positive effect on attendance, behavior, and focus. The school needs to develop partnerships with local sports programs and professional teams and with arts-related organizations.

### Telling Your Story
We serve the poorest congressional district in the United States. Many of our families live below the poverty level. The children do not have access to sports and arts programs within the school, and opportunities within the community are limited. Most of our families cannot afford to pay for private programs or even low-cost community programs. If you sponsor a sports or arts program in our school, we will be able to provide our children with a potential path to college through scholarships or admission to specialized schools.

### Establishing Strategic Partnerships
Possible partners to look into include elected officials, professional sports teams, private donors, federal government agencies, community-based organizations, local sports programs, and community centers.

## What We Learned from the Pandemic

The COVID-19 pandemic took away children's access to sports and arts programs. They did not engage in physical and creative activities, and the loss of access had a direct effect on their social and emotional needs. Physical exercise helps mitigate such mental health concerns as depression, anxiety, impulse control, and aggressiveness (Tandon et al., 2021). Likewise, arts programming over extended periods enhances children's social skills, such as sharing and cooperation, and reduces not only shyness and anxiety but also aggressive behavior (Alavinezhad et al., 2014; Menzer, 2015). In particular, children who depended on school for such programming—who didn't have the means to access it outside school—were at a steep disadvantage socially and emotionally to their higher-socioeconomic-status peers during the pandemic.

# Sample Projects

Sports and arts programs come in many forms. Here are descriptions of various projects that address this issue. They may give you ideas for how you can address this priority at your school.

### Saturday Soccer

Through a partnership with a nonprofit organization called Street Soccer USA, C.S. 55 is able to provide a soccer program for our students. The organization provides two coaches free of charge, and the school provides the space for practice and play.

### Local Baseball and Football Leagues

Local sports leagues are always looking to partner with schools to invite children and families to participate. Such programs may be fee-based, but you can look for funding sources, including professional teams, to help underwrite the costs. As an added benefit, and in response to my invitation, coaches have come to C.S. 55 to talk to students about the importance of attendance and good behavior.

### Schoolyards and Fields

Quality sports programs require adequate space. Work with elected officials, community leaders, and community-based organizations to design and fund a gym or a field. Although the primary goal is to create a space where children can run, engage in physical activity, and play sports, the community can also use this space for outdoor events and distribution of resources such as food.

### Arts Programs

Our children learn through pictures in the early grades. Art allows them to express themselves and communicate before they acquire writing skills. The arts also allow for our children to be creative and innovative. Helping students to become proficient in the arts and music gives them more opportunities to be well-rounded and successful in life; like sports programs, arts programs can lead to access to specialized schools and college scholarships. At C.S. 55, we hired a music teacher to teach students to play musical instruments. We want to instill a love of the arts in our students and encourage them to pursue careers in the arts in the future if they wish to.

## School-Based Sports Teams

Access to sports not only is about health but also can lead to entry into specialized schools and gaining scholarships to college. Students who participate in sports tend to behave better than their fellow students and gain skills necessary to be successful in the workforce. At C.S. 55, we now have competitive teams in archery, soccer, basketball, tennis, and softball. Our focus on sports has increased student and parent engagement and, as a bonus, improved student attendance, behavior, and confidence.

## Step Teams and Dance Programs

Stepping, or step dancing, is a form of synchronized dancing in which the dancers use their feet and hands to create complex rhythmic dances. Many schools have staff members or parents who were members of step teams in high school or college. Forming step teams or other dance programs is a great way to incorporate both sports and arts into your school. In my experience, stepping has a positive impact on students' morale, behavior, and attendance.

# Conclusion

From the problems of food access to the inequities that exist with technology, it is obvious that education is not—*cannot* be—the first priority for many of our families. Although this is a major challenge, many people are actively fighting to address these basic needs so that our families can focus on education.

The goal of this book is to provide you with ideas, tools, and action plans to help you take steps to address these needs. If you follow the community-matching process and you are willing to put in the work, I am certain that you will be able to support many families in your own school community in addressing these priorities so that your children and families can have access to nutritious food, adequate shelter, a safe environment, mental and physical health supports, technology, and a high-quality education. Once you become an equity warrior in this way, you will give your students a better chance at success in school and life.

# Appendix:
# Strategic Partnerships

Establishing strategic partnerships is an essential part of addressing the six priorities and developing a successful community school. Here are some ideas for finding partners who can work with you to achieve your goals.

## Community-Based Organizations

The following organizations are some of the partners I've worked with at C.S. 55. They are based in New York City and focus their support on the city's public schools. I am including them here as examples of the kinds of organizations you might look for in your community and the kinds of support they might provide.

- **BronxNet**—BronxNet is a local cable television network in the Bronx that delivers programming for education and government. Local television stations can be valuable partners in getting your message out to the greater community. These organizations can provide a platform for meetings, forums, educational programming, and more. During the pandemic, C.S. 55 was able to continue to provide educational resources to our children through BronxNet. This service was particularly valuable for children who had little or no access to computer-based technology at home. Our visibility through BronxNet also enabled us to connect with new partners.

- **Center for Educational Innovation (CEI)**—Anchored in its belief that all students deserve a quality education, CEI strengthens public education by sharing student-centered innovations and creating model schools. CEI believes the school should be the center and driving force of innovation and reform and, as such, it provides customized, school-based, embedded professional development, mentoring, and coaching to school leaders and teacher teams. Its goal is to create high-performing schools in underresourced communities to help children succeed.

- **Educators for Student Success (ESS)**—ESS is a not-for-profit company that was designed to meet the needs of schools within the New York City metropolitan area. ESS supports schools and districts with expert consultants in all areas of school operations, instruction, intervention, culture and climate, family engagement, grant application, planning, and so on. Consultants, all experts in their area of support, include former superintendents, network leaders, principals, department heads, and coaches. All support is tailored to the school or district's needs and is collaboratively negotiated.

- **Green Bronx Machine**—The Green Bronx Machine creates educational opportunities to support communities in raising awareness around and addressing major gaps in health and wellness, particularly as related to healthy food. At C.S. 55, their support for the creation of our school farm has helped our students to become productive, health-conscious citizens.

- **New York Cares**—New York Cares is a nonprofit organization that recruits and organizes volunteers for a wide range of causes, including services to senior citizens, hunger relief, health and wellness, neighborhood revitalization, and literacy and other education-related issues. At C.S. 55, we have found that partnering with organizations such as New York Cares has made our work of addressing inequities less challenging. These types of organizations are based on the idea that volunteers can play an important role in ensuring that all children and families have access to things that will help them be successful in life. Many of our partners have come to us through our involvement with New York Cares.

- **SCAN-Harbor**—SCAN-Harbor is a social-service provider for at-risk youth and their families. At C.S. 55, our collaboration with SCAN-Harbor enabled us to become a true community school by helping us establish an after-school program, start a food pantry (where many of our former students now work), and hire staff who speak the multiple languages spoken in the surrounding area.

- **Windows of Hip Hop**—Windows of Hip Hop is a nonprofit organization devoted to the history, educational value, and community impact of hip hop music. Pioneers of hip hop as well as up-and-coming artists provide high-quality instruction in spoken word, rap, deejaying, emceeing, and more. From music and fashion to art and dance, students are able to embrace the many cultural pieces that make up their identity. Windows of Hip Hop provides programming in all elements of the art form, from the clothes people wear to the business of music, from break dancing to graffiti.

## Sports Teams

All sports organizations have a community relations office with responsibilities such as distributing free tickets, issuing invitations for special events, and organizing giveaways. During the holidays, sports organizations may provide free dinners for families and holiday gifts for children. Most teams are looking for ways to partner directly with schools and organizations and also may provide many other opportunities for schools to receive funding for various projects. If you have a professional sports team in your area, you can contact the team directly. Here are links to some sites that provide more general information about sports organizations' charitable programs:

- **Major League Baseball**—www.mlb.com/mlb-community/get -involved

- **Major League Soccer**—www.mlssoccer.com/mls-works

- **National Basketball Association**—https://nbafoundation.nba.com

- **National Football League**—www.nfl.com/community

## Corporate Donors

Some large corporations have departments that make charitable contributions through grants and other resources. For example, after the nonprofit organization New York Cares informed us about a grant available from The Home Depot, C.S. 55 received $10,000 from the company that allowed us to fully furnish a library in the school. Here are just a few companies to consider reaching out to:

- **Staples**—Grants and product donations for mentoring, tutoring, college preparation, and job-skills development (www.staples.com/sbd/cre/marketing/about_us/how-we -give.html)

- **Target**—Community Engagement Funds, holiday giving, and donations through local stores (https://corporate.target.com /sustainability-esg/community-engagement/corporate-giving)

- **Walmart**—Local Community grants (https://walmart.org/how-we -give/local-community-grants)

The following companies also have philanthropic programs; visit their websites for more information: Costco, General Electric, Google, and Microsoft.

## Supporters of the Arts

Windows of Hip Hop, mentioned above, is a big part of how C.S. 55 accesses the arts. You, too, can try connecting with local arts institutions, museums, and nonprofit organizations to support your programs. The following are additional organizations and programs to help schools incorporate the arts, which are often underfunded or receive zero funding in public schools:

- **Associated Chamber Music Players**—Awards grants for ongoing programs and special projects promoting participatory chamber music activities worldwide (https://acmp.net/grants)

- **Fender Play Foundation**—Aims to increase access to music education through innovative and sustainable programs that put instruments and learning tools directly in the hands of students and teachers (https://fenderplayfoundation.org)

- **Gewirtz Fund**—Funds music programs that incorporate string music education (https://sites.google.com/site /gewirtzkidstoconcerts)

- **The Mockingbird Foundation**—Provides funding for music education for children (https://mbird.org/grants)

- **National Art Education Foundation**—Provides grants to support instructional practice, research, and leadership in visual arts education (www.arteducators.org/opportunities/national-art -education-foundation)

- **Save the Music Foundation**—Partners with school districts and local communities to build sustainable music programs (www.savethemusic.org)

## Other Sources

- **AdoptAClassroom**—Crowdfunding platform enabling educators to request resources and materials for their classrooms (www.adoptaclassroom.org)

- **DonorsChoose**—A nonprofit that allows individuals to respond directly to public school teachers' requests for funding for classroom projects (www.donorschoose.org)

- **Fundly**—Information on corporate giving at more than 90 companies, with guidance on how to make an appeal and raise funds (https://blog.fundly.com/donation-requests)
- **Double the Donation**—Information on corporate giving at more than 45 companies (https://doublethedonation.com/tips /donation-requests)

# References

Alavinezhad, R., Mousavi, M., & Sohrabi, N. (2014). Effects of art therapy on anger and self-esteem in aggressive children. *Procedia—Social and Behavioral Sciences, 113,* 111–117.

Atske, S., & Perrin, A. (2021). *Home broadband adoption, computer ownership vary by race, ethnicity in the U.S.* Pew Research Center. www.pewresearch .org/fact-tank/2021/07/16/home-broadband-adoption-computer -ownership-vary-by-race-ethnicity-in-the-u-s

Caughron, J. R. (2016). *An examination of food insecurity and its impact on violent crime in American communities.* All Theses. 2565. https:// tigerprints.clemson.edu/all_theses/2565

Coalition for the Homeless. (2022, March). *Basic facts about homelessness: New York City.* www.coalitionforthehomeless.org/basic-facts-about -homelessness-new-york-city

Freitag, E. (2021, July 6). The pandemic will worsen our reading problem. Another outcome is possible. *Education Week.* www.edweek.org/teaching -learning/opinion-the-pandemic-will-worsen-illiteracy-another-outcome -is-possible/2021/07

Green Bronx Machine. (n.d.). *The National Health, Wellness, and Learning Center at CS 55.* https://greenbronxmachine.org/projects/the-national -health-and-wellness-center-at-ps-55

Henry, M., de Sousa T., Roddey, C., Gayen, S., & Bednar, T. J. (2021, January). *The 2020 annual homeless assessment report (AHAR) to Congress: Part 1: Point-in-time estimates of homelessness.* U.S. Department of

Housing and Urban Development. www.huduser.gov/portal/sites
/default/files/pdf/2020-AHAR-Part-1.pdf

Hudson, J. (2012, July 2). An urban myth that should be true. *The Atlantic.*
www.theatlantic.com/business/archive/2012/07/an-urban-myth-that
-should-be-true/259329

Johnston, W. R., Engberg, J., Opper, I. M., Sontag-Padilla, L., & Xenakis, L.
(n.d.). *Illustrating the promise of community schools: An assessment of
the impact of the New York City Community Schools Initiative.* RAND
Corporation. www.rand.org/pubs/research_reports/RR3245.html

Menzer, M. (2015). *The arts in early childhood: Social and emotional benefits
of arts participation. A literature review and gap-analysis (2000–2015).*
Office of Research & Analysis, National Endowment for the Arts.
www.americansforthearts.org/sites/default/files/arts-in-early-childhood
-dec2015-rev.pdf

National Center for Education Statistics (NCES). (2017). Table 204.10.
Number and percentage of public school students eligible for free or
reduced-price lunch, by state: Selected years, 2000–01 through 2015–16.
*Digest of Education Statistics.* https://nces.ed.gov/programs/digest/d17
/tables/dt17_204.10.asp

New York City Department of Education. (n.d.). *NYC Community Schools.*
www.schools.nyc.gov/learning/programs/community-schools

Office of Community Food Systems. (2021). *School gardens: Using gardens
to grow healthy habits in cafeterias, classrooms, and communities.* U.S.
Department of Agriculture. https://fns-prod.azureedge.us/sites/default
/files/resource-files/USDA_OCFS_FactSheet_SchoolGardens_508.pdf

Tandon, P. S., Zhou, C., Johnson, A. M., Schoenfelder Gonzalez, E., &
Kroshus, E. (2021). Association of children's physical activity and screen
time with mental health during the COVID-19 pandemic. *JAMA Network
Open, 4*(10). https://jamanetwork.com/journals/jamanetworkopen
/fullarticle/2784611

Turner, S. D. (2016). *Digital denied: The impact of systemic racial discrimination
on home-internet adoption.* Free Press.

# Index

The letter f following a page number denotes a figure.

# About the Author

 **Luis Eladio Torres** is the president of the New York City Elementary School Principals Association, District 9 Executive Board representative, and chairperson of the Bronx Elementary School Principals Consortium. He has served as a school principal in New York City for more than 18 years.

After serving in the U.S. Navy for 10 years, Torres earned an associate's degree in biology from Hostos Community College, a bachelor's degree in psychology from the City College of New York, a master's degree in education from Mercy College, and an advanced degree in administration from Hunter College. Torres then entered the New York City Leadership Academy, after which he was given the responsibility of leading C.S. 55 in the Bronx. Torres and his team are responsible for turning C.S. 55—once the lowest-performing school in New York City, located in District 9 in the center of the Morrisania housing projects in the Bronx—into a model school. Torres has raised millions of dollars for C.S. 55 and surrounding schools, acting as his school's spokesperson, publicist, and cheerleader.

Torres's efforts have now shifted to Whole Community Education, with a focus on improving the conditions of the community. He has a unique connection with this community because he is a product of the New York City public school system as well as the Bronx. Torres's father, Angel Luis Torres, an apartment building superintendent and a community organizer, raised him to be a leader in the community and to give back. When his father passed away, Torres made a commitment to continue the work his father started.

Torres lives in the Bronx with his wife, Joan Torres, and their three children, who have all attended or are attending district schools.

# Related ASCD Resources

At the time of publication, the following resources were available (ASCD stock numbers appear in parentheses).

*Aim High, Achieve More: How to Transform Urban Schools Through Fearless Leadership* by Yvette Jackson and Veronica McDermott (#112015)

*Create Success! Unlocking the Potential of Urban Students* by Kadhir Rajagopal (#111022)

*Culture, Class, and Race: Constructive Conversations That Unite and Energize Your School and Community* by Brenda CampbellJones, Shannon Keeny, and Franklin CampbellJones (#118010)

*Is My School a Better Place Because I Lead It?* by Baruti K. Kafele (#120013)

*Meeting Students Where They Live: Motivation in Urban Schools* by Richard L. Curwin (#109110)

*Mobilizing the Community to Help Students Succeed* by Hugh B. Price (#107055)

*Restoring Students' Innate Power: Trauma-Responsive Strategies for Teaching Multilingual Newcomers* by Louise El Yaafouri (#122004)

*Teaching and Supporting Students Living with Adversity* (Quick Reference Guide) by Debbie Zacarian and Lourdes Alvarez-Ortiz (#QRG120035)

*Trauma-Sensitive School Leadership: Building a Learning Environment to Support Healing and Success* by Bill Ziegler, Dave Ramage, Andrea Parson, and Justin Foster (#122013)

*Turning High-Poverty Schools into High-Performing Schools, 2nd Edition* by William H. Parrett and Kathleen M. Budge (#120031)

For up-to-date information about ASCD resources, go to **www.ascd.org**. You can search the complete archives of *Educational Leadership* at **www.ascd.org/el**.

## ASCD myTeachSource®

Download resources from a professional learning platform with hundreds of research-based best practices and tools for your classroom at http:// myteachsource.ascd.org/.

For more information, send an email to member@ascd.org; call 1-800-933-2723 or 703-578-9600; send a fax to 703-575-5400; or write to Information Services, ASCD, 2800 Shirlington Road, Suite 1001, Arlington, VA 22206 USA.

# CHILD

The ASCD Whole Child approach is an effort to transition from a focus on narrowly defined academic achievement to one that promotes the long-term development and success of all children. Through this approach, ASCD supports educators, families, community members, and policymakers as they move from a vision about educating the whole child to sustainable, collaborative actions.

*The Six Priorities* relates to all five tenets.

*For more about the ASCD Whole Child approach, visit* **www.ascd.org/wholechild.**

## WHOLE CHILD
# TENETS

**1 HEALTHY**
Each student enters school healthy and learns about and practices a healthy lifestyle.

**2 SAFE**
Each student learns in an environment that is physically and emotionally safe for students and adults.

**3 ENGAGED**
Each student is actively engaged in learning and is connected to the school and broader community.

**4 SUPPORTED**
Each student has access to personalized learning and is supported by qualified, caring adults.

**5 CHALLENGED**
Each student is challenged academically and prepared for success in college or further study and for employment and participation in a global environment.